Benjamin Hall Kennedy

The Birds of Aristophanes

Benjamin Hall Kennedy

The Birds of Aristophanes

ISBN/EAN: 9783337042639

Printed in Europe, USA, Canada, Australia, Japan

Cover: Foto ©ninafisch / pixelio.de

More available books at **www.hansebooks.com**

THE BIRDS OF ARISTOPHANES

TRANSLATED INTO ENGLISH VERSE

WITH

INTRODUCTION, NOTES, AND
APPENDICES

BY

BENJAMIN HALL KENNEDY, D.D.,
REGIUS PROFESSOR OF GREEK IN THE UNIVERSITY OF CAMBRIDGE.

London:
MACMILLAN AND CO.
1874.

[*All Rights reserved.*]

MEMORIAE · AETERNAE

EDVARDI · GEORGII · LYTTON · BVLVER · LYTTON

BARONIS · LYTTON

QVI · CLARIS · NATALIBVS · AMPLIS · FORTVNIS · INGENIO · SVMMO

SINGVLARI · TAMEN · INDVSTRIA · FVIT

ET · BONARVM · ARTIVM · STVDIIS · A · PVERITIA · DEDITVS

QVI · CVM · SCRIPTOR · IN · OMNI · FERE · LITTERARVM · GENERE

INTER · SAECVLI · SVI · PRINCIPES · ELVCERET

CVM · IN · CONCILIO · POPVLI · IS · ESSET · ORATOR

VT · ELOQVENTIA · SVA · OMNIVM · AVRES · TENERET

CVM · REGINAE · ESSET · A · SECRETIS · CONSILIIS

ET · COLONIIS · ADMINISTRANDIS · QVONDAM · PRAEPOSITVS

ILLVD · TAMEN · TOT · LAVDIBVS · ADIVNXIT

VT · AMICVS · ESSE · POSSET · OFFICIOSVS · LIBERALIS · FIDELIS

HVNC · QVALEMCVMQVE · LIBRVM

DESIDERIO · TANTI · VIRI · PERCITVS

ET · AMICITIAE · MEMOR

PER · ANNOS · VNDEQVINQVAGINTA · PRODVCTAE

D. D.

B. H. KENNEDY

IN · ACADEMIA · CANTABR. GRAEC. LITT. PROFESSOR · REGIVS

TO

ROBERT, LORD LYTTON,

&c., &c., &c.

MY DEAR LORD LYTTON,

The Translation of *The Birds* of Aristophanes which, with Introduction and Notes, appears in this volume, is the outgrowth of Lectures delivered by me as Greek Professor in this University. When I first thought of printing it, my chief motive was that, by dedicating it to your father, I might express the value I set on the constant friendship with which he had honoured me from our College days. But it was not ordered that he should see this expression of my feeling. His illustrious life was brought to a close within the first weeks of 1873; and to me, his elder in age by a few months, it was left to say mournfully, 'i prae; sequar.'

You, of whom as his son and successor he was justly proud, kindly promised to represent him by accepting the dedication of this book. When I asked of you that favour, I thought it likely that I should wish to say something of your father's place in the literary and political history of his time. But I have abandoned that design, as too delicate to be now undertaken, and too difficult for me to undertake. What I would not willingly leave unsaid, you will see on another page, in the concise form of a Latin inscription. Perhaps some future historian, writing with impartial pen, may combine that testimony with his other materials, when he comes to treat of the life and writings of Edward, first Lord Lytton.

Permit me to say a few words about the present work.

My wish has been to produce a translation of *The Birds* which may be agreeable to the taste of English readers, and make the genius of Aristophanes and the character of his age more familiar to their minds. For this purpose I have chosen English metres, which in some instances are those of the original, but generally differ from them. German translators adhere to the Greek rhythms; and I suppose therefore that to some modern ears the result is gratifying. Mine are not among the number. Few of our countrymen, I fancy, would in the dialogue prefer a series of heavy Alexandrine lines to the usual ten-syllable measure of the English drama. And still less tolerable in our language would be the attempt to imitate the lyric metres of the Greek.

In writing Greek proper names I have followed the practice of Mr Grote. I do not forget that, by so doing,

I lay myself open to the humorous and good-tempered criticism of your father in 'The Caxtons.' But I disclaim all pedantic preference in this matter. Horace, Virgil, Livy, Aristotle, and other cropt names I use as everybody else does in familiar writing and parlance. But in a history or a translation, where the purpose is mainly to carry the reader's mind back to ancient times and scenes, it is surely right to avoid those distortions of sound in old names which leave the mind under an erroneous impression. How can we without absurdity call the son of Miltiades (Kīmon) by the title of Sīmon, thus confounding him with St Peter, or with the magician who has given name to the offence of simony? I go as far as Mr Grote has gone, but no farther. He does not write the ending -os, but -us; not Athenae, but Athens; not Peisandrus, Alexandrus, Philippus, but Peisander, Alexander, Philip: and in many other instances he defers, and I with him, to that inconsistent but all-powerful dictator, Custom,

> Quem penes arbitrium est et ius et norma loquendi.

Believe me,

My dear Lord Lytton,

With sincere thanks,

Yours very faithfully,

B. H. KENNEDY.

THE ELMS, CAMBRIDGE,
June 1st, 1874.

INTRODUCTION.

§ 1. THE origin of the Greek drama, comic as well as tragic, is traced to the festivals of the Wine-god Dionysus or Bacchus. All such feasts were naturally mirthful; some were licentious also. In those frequented by the higher classes, a Chorus danced round the altar of the god, singing lyric songs, called 'dithyrambic,' in which were celebrated the legends of Dionysus, with the praises of the vine and its produce. A recitative by a single actor, addressed to the spectators in the intervals between these songs, was the first step in the gradual development of the Greek tragic drama. The choral dancers were disguised as Satyrs, the merry goat-footed companions of the wine-god. Hence, probably, and not, as many have supposed, from a goat-sacrifice or a goat-prize, arose the name of Tragedy, Tragoedia or Goat-song. Hence, too, in the tragic contests at Athens, one of the four plays produced by each competing poet was a drama called Satyric, in which the Chorus consisted of Satyrs. Such is *The Cyclops*, which appears among the works of Euripides.

Here we quit the topic of Greek Tragedy. The works of K. O. Müller and Mure on Greek Literature,

The Greek Theatre by Donaldson, and the *Grecian Histories* of Thirlwall, Grote and E. Curtius, supply ample information on this subject. See also *The Greek Poets*, by Mr J. A. Symonds, a truly genial volume, not less interesting than instructive, from which, by the author's kind permission, some extracts appear in this Introduction.

§ 2. The more licentious festivals were those of the vintage, celebrated by the rural population. In these the singing and dancing were often of a riotous and ribald character. The phallus-emblem was carried in procession, and extolled, as the comrade of Bacchus, in songs called phallic or ithyphallic, of which a specimen exists in Aristophanes (*Acharn.* 261—279). The procession of choral revellers (Komus) went in carts from house to house, from village to village; and their songs alternated with the speech of a single actor, who, in order to amuse the rustic crowds and provoke their laughter, assailed with scandalous ridicule and grotesque caricature all persons present or absent, all things sacred or profane, from which materials could be drawn to serve his purpose. Such was the origin of Comedy, Comoedia, the Komus-song: an explanation now justly preferred to that of Village-song, by which, as Aristotle says (*Poet.* III), the Dorians, who called a village Komê, supported their claim to the invention of the comic drama. Hence the verb 'komoedein' (to comoedize) means 'to ridicule' or 'caricature[1].' Another name

[1] The verb 'iambizein' (to iambize) has a similar meaning; but it has no relation to Dionysus or the drama, although the 'iambic'

designating Comedy is Trugoedia, the song of the Truges or Wine-lees, with which the vintagers, when singing and acting, reddened their faces; though some, less probably, suppose this term to imply a prize of rich wine bestowed on the best singer or actor. In the vintage-songs, then, we find the original of the comic chorus; and in the interlude of the actor the primal germ both of the dialogue and also of the comic parabasis, the railing parts being especially represented by the pungent allusions usually contained in the epirrhema and antepirrhema. See Appendix.

§ 3. The growth of Comedy was slower and its development later than that of Tragedy. Its first appearance in Greece is assigned by Aristotle (*Poet.* III) to the small Doric state of Megaris, between Attika and the Peloponnese: and the phaenomenon is ascribed to the license of democratic polity. Hence Meineke fixes the date of this comic outburst about the 43rd or 44th Olympiad, after the expulsion of Theagenes, tyrant of Megara, who had assisted his son-in-law Kylon in his attempt on the Athenian Akropolis. The Megarian comic poet of that age (about B.C. 600) was Susarion of Tripodiskus, son of Philinus, who is said by scholiasts

became the metre of dramatic dialogue. Legend refers it, but without probability, to the mysteries of Demeter. There is more historic truth in the tradition which ascribes to Archilochus the invention of iambic rhythm, and its application to the purpose of invective. 'Archilochum proprio rabies armavit iambo,' says Horace. But here, as often, the exact truth cannot be discovered through the dimness of the past.—See K. O. Müller, *Hist. of Gr. Lit.* ch. XI. § 5.

to have transferred his stage to the Ikarian borough within the confines of Attika, where the rustic rites of Dionysus were specially renowned (Meineke, *Hist. Com. Gr.* I. 48). Susarion is cited as the first comic author who composed metrically and not extemporaneously. Megarian comedy was noted for the broadness and coarseness of its humour. A Megarian jest became proverbial; and Aristophanes in *The Wasps* (v. 57) disclaims the intention of stealing his wit from Megara. The names of Maeson, Mullus, and a few more, are recorded as having produced comedies in the Megarian manner after Susarion.

§ 4. Comedy is next heard of in Sicily, the Megarians of Greece having probably conveyed it to their Sicilian colony, the Hyblaean Megara. Aristotle and others mention the comic poet Phormis or Phormus, who was tutor to the children of Gelon at Syracuse. Junior to him, but far more illustrious, was Epicharmus, a native of Kos, whose father Helothales migrated from that island to Sicily when his son was an infant. Epicharmus was renowned not only in comedy, but also in medicine (being probably one of the Koan Asklepiads) and in the Pythagorean philosophy. He lived to extreme old age, as late as the 84th Olympiad, but his poetic fame belongs chiefly to the years B.C. 500—480. His plays were various in subject and style: some mythic caricatures, as *The Busiris* and *The Hephaestus;* others portraying character and manners in a philosophic spirit, as *The Agrostinus* or Countryman; others treating of historic or political matter in a similar spirit, as *The Harpagae* (Plunderings) and *The Nasoi* (Islands). His only successor in Sicilian comedy was Deinolochus, who is variously represented as his son and as his disciple. But about fifty years later the Sicilian Sophron excelled in a species of drama called Mimes. These dealt with manners and morals; but K. O. Müller (*Dorians* VII.) thinks they were not brought on the stage. The reputation of Epicharmus in Greece was very high; Plato (*Theaet.*) says that he was pre-eminent in his own poetic sphere, as Homer in the Epic. See Bernhardy, (*Gr. Lit.* II. 454, &c.).

§ 5. The tragic drama was theatrically represented at Athens at least fifty years before Comedy was recognized there by legal provision for the maintenance of a chorus (choragia). Aristotle mentions, as the earliest poets of the old comedy at Athens, Chionides and Magnes, with whom must be joined the name of Ekphantides. It is very improbable that they were actively at work before the close of the Persian Wars B.C. 479: but Grote is hardly right in placing them so late as the 80th Olympiad, B.C. 460. Their immediate successors were the famous Kratinus, whom the Latin poet Persius aptly calls 'the bold,' and Krates, to whom the organism of the comic stage was probably indebted for improvement. Kratinus it was, we cannot doubt, who, if not first, yet most vigorously and successfully, asserted for a comic poet the right of speaking as a 'censor morum,' a critic and a judge of morals public and private. The dramatic career of Kratinus, which did not cease till his death B.C. 423, began as early as the 82nd Olympiad at latest: and we may well suppose that the virulence of his ridicule occasioned the enactment of the law B. C. 440, which forbade the introduction of living characters in comedy. This law was repealed within two years: and the high-minded Perikles, in his administration, bore unflinchingly the pelting of the pitiless comic storm in the yearly contests of the Wine-god: thus manifesting his moral courage, his just self-reliance, his confidence in the good sense of the people, and his reverence for poetic art.

§ 6. "The Old Comedy" (says E. Curtius), "drawing its topics of censure from present society and every-day life, could exercise influence and achieve success in no condition but that of unrestrained democracy, which it attends through every grade of development. Occupied from the first with the ridiculous in human action and character, it chastised with a keen scourge all errors, follies and weaknesses, of which it found an ample store in a society so busy and conspicuous as that of Athens, having an audience alive to wit and prone to laughter, ready to understand and enjoy every allusion, even when conveyed with the most covert irony. All abuses and inconsistencies of public as well as private life were exposed to the comic lash. This the poet regarded as his grandest function. Without the stimulus of a great patriotic purpose, his work would have seemed to him a mere tissue of jokes and gibes, poor and despicable. His design was not to amuse only, but also to instruct and guide the people; and in this object Comedy shewed itself a true sister of Tragedy."

Bernhardy says (II. 961):

"The Old Comedy has a political character; it exercises the functions of a political censorship, and also, like a powerful pamphlet, it asserts public opinion for the first time with unfettered freedom of speech. Every one of its Plays throws light on the social condition of the State in some one important particular, holding up at the same time a mirror in which is reflected the general character of the whole."

§ 7. This boldness of the Old Attic Comedy grew out of the consciousness of its peculiar origin. It knew itself descended from a Bacchanalian chorus of rustics, full of new wine: a chorus, whose motto was free licence, whose rule was to be without rule; who sang improvised songs of reverence or ribaldry, in which the beautiful sank to the base and the base rose to the beautiful in strange alternation: whose mimic dances were graceful or indecorous as the feeling of the moment prompted; who, when song and dance flagged, could listen with keen delight to the cleverest and wittiest of their crew, as, mounted on a cart, he showered around, in extempore recitative, his darts of unbridled and unsparing ridicule, which sparkled as they flew, and stung wherever they fell. All these things—song, dance, and recitation—we find comprised in any perfect parabasis of the Attic Comedy. The parabasis is the nucleus around which the other parts have grown. The plot, the action, all that is properly called drama, is an artistic development, achieved by the genius and skill of successive poets, to whom we cannot, for want of accurate information, assign the shares severally due.

§ 8. To the Old Attic Comedy may be ascribed a duration of about eighty years, ending with the Second *Plutus* of Aristophanes, B.C. 389, which marks the transition to the Middle Comedy. But its flourishing period cannot be estimated at more than fifty-six years, ending with the capture of Athens by Lysander B.C. 404. The Middle Comedy of Athens was itself superseded by the New (of Menander, Philemon, and Diphilus) about the time of Alexander's death, B.C. 323. Forty poets (didaskaloi) of the Old Comedy are recorded by grammarians and biographers. The three most eminent of these are linked in fame by Horace,

> Eupolis atque Cratinus Aristophanesque poetae.
> *Sat.* I. iv. 1.

Persius places them in just chronological order:

> Audaci quicumque afflate Cratino
> Iratum Eupolidem praegrandi cum sene palles.
> I. 123.

Of the rest, those who deserve special notice[1] are Krates (see § 5), Pherekrates, Telekleides, Hermippus, Phrynichus, Ameipsias (whose *Komastae* gained the prize against *The Birds* of Aristophanes), Plato (Comicus), Theopompus and Strattis. The last three continued to compose in the Middle Comedy also. The titles of about 390 comedies of these authors are handed down: the fragments of which are collected and arranged by Meineke, *Fragm. Com. Gr.* The only perfect works are the eleven plays of Aristophanes.

§ 9. Little is known of the life of Aristophanes; and that little is chiefly drawn from his extant works. Even the dates of his birth and death are uncertain.

---

[1] The full list is: Chionides, Magnes, Ekphantides, Kratinus, Krates, Pherekrates, Telekleides, Hermippus, Myrtilus, Eupolis, Philonides, Phrynichus, Aristophanes, Ameipsias, Archippus, Aristomenes, Kallias, Lysippus, Leukon, Metagenes, Aristagoras, Plato, Theopompus, Strattis, Aristonymus, Alkaeus, Eunikus, Kantharus, Diokles, Nikochares, Nikophon, Philyllius, Polyzelus, Sannyrion, Apollophanes, Epilykus, Euthykles, Demetrius, Kephisodorus, Autokrates.—See Meineke, I.; Bernhardy, *Gr. Lit.* II. 515, &c. On Magnes, Kratinus and Krates, see *The Knights*, vv. 520—544.

INTRODUCTION. xvii

For the former B.C. 452 and B.C. 448 are suggested by different scholars, for the latter B.C. 380. His father's name was Philippus, who seems to have been a landed proprietor in the isle of Aegina, and some think the poet was born there; which will account, in this view, for his strong disposition to be at peace with the Peloponnesians. Fifty-four comedies are ascribed to him by some biographers, of which Bergk allows forty-three only to be genuine. See B. ap. Mein. *Fr. Com. Gr.* II. p. 2. Some of these were exhibited under the names of Kallistratus and Philonides, most in his own name. His first play, *The Banqueters*, was acted B.C. 428 (Clinton 427) in the name of Philonides. It was designed to ridicule and reprobate degenerate novelties in education at Athens. In the next year appeared *The Babylonians*, directed against the vices of election to office by lot. This is said to have provoked against Kallistratus, in whose name it appeared, a process conducted by Kleon without success.

§ 10. The extant Comedies appeared in the following order :—

1. B.C. 426 (Cl. 425). *The Acharnians*, condemning the war policy of Athens (in the name of Kallistratus).
2. B.C. 425 (Cl. 424). *The Knights*, assailing the person and policy of Kleon.
3. B.C. 424 (Cl. 423). *The* (first) *Clouds*, against the Sophists impersonated in Sokrates.
4. B.C. 423 (Cl. 422). *The Wasps*, against the litigation prevalent at Athens (in the name of Philonides).
5. B.C. 422 (Cl. 419). *The Peace;* fable of its conclusion and rejoicings thereon.
6. B.C. 414. *The Birds*, during the Sicilian expedition : scope questionable (in the name of Kallistratus).

b

7. B.C. 411. *Lysistrata;* against the war, from women's point of view.

8. B.C. 411. *Thesmophoriazusae;* ridicule of Agathon, of Euripides, and of women.

[B.C. 408. *The* (first) *Plutus*].

9. B.C. 405. *The Frogs;* dramatic criticism, extolling Aeschylus, censuring Euripides.

10. B.C. 393 (Cl. 392). *Ekklesiazusae;* new social system under female laws.

11. B.C. 389 (Cl. 388). *The* (second) *Plutus;* redistribution of wealth on the principle of merit.

§ 11. The personal character of Aristophanes was evidently respected by his contemporaries. In proof of this, we need only cite Plato, who, in his Dialogue called *The Symposium*, gives an honourable place beside his master Sokrates to the very comic poet, who had covered that master and his school with ridicule in *The Clouds*. The splendour of his genius is said to be commemorated by the same great philosopher, in the epigram which one of the poet's biographers has preserved :—

"The Graces sought a shrine which ne'er should fall,
And found the soul of Aristophanes."

§ 12. The character of his genius and style is admirably portrayed by Mr Symonds (*The Greek Poets*, p. 234, &c.) :—

"In approaching Aristophanes we must divest our minds of all the ordinary canons and definitions of Comedy: we must forget what we have learned from Plautus and Terence, from Molière and Jonson. No modern poet, except perhaps Shakespeare and Calderon in parts, will help us to understand him. We must not expect to find the gist of Aristophanes in vivid portraits of character, in situations borrowed from every-day life, in witty dialogues, in carefully constructed plots arriving at felicitous conclusions. All these elements, indeed, he has,—but these are not the main points of his art. His plays are not comedies in the sense in which we use the word, but scenic allegories; Titanic farces in which the whole world is turned upside down; transcendental travesties, enormous orgies of wild fancy and unbridled imagination, Dionysiac dances in which tears are mingled with laughter, and fire with wine; choruses that, underneath their oceanic merriment of leaping waves, hide silent deeps of unstirred thought. If Coleridge was justified in claiming the word *Lustpiel* for the so-called comedies of Shakespeare, we have a far greater right to appropriate this wide and pregnant title to the plays of Aristophanes. . . . . . Nor is it only by this unearthly splendour of visionary loveliness that Aristophanes attracts us. Beauty of a more mundane and sensual sort is his. Multitudes of brilliant ever-changing figures fill the scene; and here and there we find a landscape or a piece of music and moonlight glowing with the presence of the vintage-god. Bacchic processions of young men and maidens move before us, tossing inspired heads wreathed with jasmine flowers and wet with wine. The Mystae in the meadows of Elysium dance their rounds with the clash of cymbals and with madly twinkling snow-white feet. We catch glimpses at intervals of Athenian banquets, of midnight serenades, of the palaestra with its crowd of athletes, of the Panathenaic festival as Pheidias carved it, of all the busy rhythmic-coloured life of Greece. . . . . Aristophanes was preserved in his integrity, we need not doubt, because he shone forth as a *poet* transcendent for his splendour even among the most brilliant of Attic playwrights. Cratinus may have equalled or surpassed him in keen satire: Eupolis may have rivalled him in exquisite artistic structure; but Aristophanes must have eclipsed them, not merely by uniting their qualities successfully, but also by the exhibition of some diviner faculty, some higher spiritual afflatus. . . . . Aristophanes is a poet as Shelley or Ariosto or Shakespeare is a poet, far more than as Sophocles or Pindar or Lucretius is a poet. In spite of his profound art, we seem to hear him uttering his 'native woodnotes wild.' The subordination of the fancy to the fixed aims of the reason, which characterizes classical poetry, is not at first sight striking in Aristophanes; but he splendidly exhibits the wealth, luxuriance, variety and subtlety of the fancy working with the reason, and sometimes superseding it, which we recognize in the greatest modern poets. . . . . . . Perhaps the most splendid passages of true poetry in Aristophanes are the choruses of the initiated in *The Frogs*, the chorus of *The Clouds* before they appear upon the stage, the invitation to the nightingale and the parabasis in *The Birds*, the speech of Dikaios Logos in *The Clouds*, some of the praises of rustic life in *The Peace*, the serenade (notwithstanding its coarse satire) in *The Ecclesiazusae*, and the songs of Spartan and Athenian maidens in *The Lysistrata*. The charm of these marvellous lyrical episodes consists of their perfect simplicity and freedom. They seem to be poured forth as 'profuse strains of unpremeditated art' from the fulness of the poet's soul. Their language is elastic, changeful, finely-tempered, fitting the delicate thought like a veil of woven air. It has no Pindaric involution, no Aeschylean pompousness, no studied Sophoclean subtlety, no Euripidean *concetti*. It is always bright and Attic, sparkling like the many-twinkling laughter of the breezy sea, or like the light of morning upon rain-washed olive branches. But this poetry is never very deep or passionate. It cannot stir us with the intensity of Sappho, with the fire and madness of the highest inspiration. Indeed, the conditions of Comedy precluded Aristophanes, even had he desired it, which we have no reason to suspect, from attempting the more august movements of lyric poetry. The peculiar glories of his style are its untutored beauties, the improvised perfection and unerring exactitude of natural expression, for which it is unparalleled by that of any other Greek poet. In her most delightful moments the muse of Aristophanes suggests an almost plaintive pathos, as if behind the comic mask there were a thinking, feeling human soul; as if the very uproar of the Bacchic merriment implied some afterthought of sadness."

§ 13. The same eloquent writer—after slightly alluding to the trite and familiar topics of Aristophanic lore, and affirming that, hackneyed as these are, Aristophanes has never been really appreciated at his worth except by a few scholars and enthusiastic poets—proceeds to assign reasons for this want of intelligence in his case. Among those reasons he specially dwells on one as the most influential: 'It is hard,' he says, 'for the modern Christian world to tolerate his freedom of speech and coarseness.' Mr Symonds treats this delicate question with consummate skill, and his discussion of it (pp. 238—246) may be commended to the careful attention of our readers; though to cite it at full lies beyond the scope of this Introduction. The truth of the matter is, that grossness was to Aristophanes a necessary element of his dramatic art. The Old Comedy was the child and representative of free Bacchic licence, re-appearing twice a-year at the Athenian festivals of Dionysus, the Dionysia of the city in March, and the Lenaea in January. Aristophanes, a comic poet by profession, competing for a prize, which his tribe, his choragus, and his own credit, spurred him on to win, could not afford to withhold from the Athenian crowds—inebriate with the loose merriment of the feasts, which were as much a part of their religion as Christmas and Easter are of ours—that high-spiced seasoning of indelicate ribaldry, which they deemed essential to the completeness of Comedy as well as to the fun of the time and their own lawful enjoyment. The tragedy of *Hamlet* with the part of Hamlet left out, a play of Etherege or Wycherley without the libertinism which a licentious age expected and relished, the pranks of Punch moralized to the taste of Hannah More, a modern pantomime omitting the clown with his jests and tricks—none of these things would be more incongruous than one of the old Attic comedies without a certain sprinkling of indecent humour. If the wreck of ages had spared to us the plays of Kratinus and Ameipsias, which were judged superior to *The Clouds*, and *The Komastae* of Ameipsias, which gained the first prize against *The Birds*, we may shrewdly suspect that among the merits of the winning comedies would be found their larger and bolder coarseness. By their free infusion of this element it is probable that *The Acharnians* and *The Knights* secured the victory: and the defeat of his finest work, *The Birds*, may have impelled Aristophanes to bid for popular favour by the more impure excesses of *The Lysistrata* and *The Thesmophoriazusae*. Such, in heathen days, at two seasons of the year, were the spectacles of the Athenians, whose women and children were excluded from the theatre. Whether times and nations nominally Christian have a just right to boast themselves in comparison with those heathens, is a problem for the historian and the moralist to settle between them. There may be some truth in the remark of Rötscher (*Aristophanes und sein Zeitalter*, p. 39) that

"the very people whose plays and poems are of the most frivolous kind, turn away with most disgust from works of art, in which sensuality preserves its real form, because their own propensities and habits are therein divested of their fair outside, and shewn in natural and naked ugliness. Their dislike of such works is but another name for the unwillingness to behold their own nature stript of all hypocritical disguise."

§ 14. It remains to consider Aristophanes as a politician. On this subject we have an extensive literature, German, English and French. Most of its writers are favourable to the poet; among the Germans, Ranke, Bergk, Meineke, E. Curtius, K. O. Müller,

Klein, etc.; in England, Bishop Thirlwall, in his *History of Greece*, ch. xxxii., and Bishop Cotton (Aristophanes, in the *Dictionary of Greek and Roman Biogr. and Mythol.*). On the other side, a host in himself, though not alone (see Droysen's Version, and Müller-Strübing, *Aristophanes und die Historische Kritik*), stands Mr Grote, who, in his *History of Greece* (Part II. ch. lxvii.), as a champion of Kleon and of Sokrates, passes sentence of condemnation on our poet as a reckless and mischievous, though highly ingenious, calumniator and libeller. After studying the comedies themselves and their contemporary history, and comparing the elaborate judgments of Thirlwall on the one side and Grote on the other, the careful student will probably see, with Mr Symonds,

"that a middle course must be followed between the extremes of regarding Aristophanes as an indecent parasite pandering to the worst inclinations of the Athenian rabble, and of looking upon him as a profound philosopher and sober patriot."

§ 15. Political feeling and action were essential to Aristophanes. He was a citizen of Athens. He reached manhood at a time when Athens had a purely democratic constitution. All public questions of chief moment were decided by the votes of the Ekklesia, or Assembly of the people; and in this Assembly every citizen of man's estate had not only a right, but a rule of duty directing him, to attend and vote. Aristophanes was a politician, therefore, were it only because he was a citizen. But more than this—he was a man of genius and literary accomplishment: he was by nature and habit a thinker and a comic poet. How could such a man, in such a state as Athens, be without political the virulent and scornful enmity with which on every occasion he assails the Sophists and Rhetoricians of his time, the innovators in literature, morals and education. Gorgias, Prodikus, and other lecturers of this class, fall under his lash; the cloudy thoughts and flimsy language of the dithyrambic versifiers, especially of Kinesias, are mercilessly caricatured. The conceited tragedies of Agathon are covered with ridicule. But the *bête noire* of Aristophanes in literature is Euripides; in education, Sokrates. Euripides, the pupil of Anaxagoras, and dramatic representative of the Rhetorical school, the poet of whining pathos, captious subtleties, and cavilling morality, is pursued by Aristophanes even after death with unsparing persiflage and keen invective. Dikaiopolis, in *The Acharnians*, sues to him for the cast-off rags of his lachrymose and mendicant heroes. In *The Thesmophoriazusae*, where the women conspire to punish him for his libels on the female sex, the scenes and sayings of his tragedies are parodied in the most absurd fashion. The comedy of *The Frogs*, which Droysen justly commends as second in merit to *The Birds* alone, was produced in the year after the death of Euripides. Dionysus, the tutelary god of the drama, undertakes to recover for the desolate stage a tragic poet from the shadowy realm. He descends thither with a prejudice and (as it would seem) a promise in favour of Euripides. But Aeschylus occupies the tragic throne below, and will not resign it to the younger rival, whose claim he despises. A literary contest ensues, in which hard and fierce words are exchanged between the

angry bards, Dionysus sitting as judge. The result
deceives the high-raised hopes of Euripides. 'Remember,' cries he, 'the gods by whom you swore to carry me
back.' 'My tongue hath sworn,' says Dionysus, 'but
Aeschylus I shall choose,' cruelly parodying a verse of
Euripides himself,

"The tongue hath sworn, the mind remains unsworn."

§ 18. What the drama of *The Knights* was for
Kleon, and *The Frogs* for Euripides, Aristophanes intended *The Clouds* to be for Sokrates—a comic pillory.
The high-born youth of Athens, with Alkibiades at their
head, flocked for conversational instruction to the lectures
of that great man, who knew how to teach winningly
and effectually, by a catechetic method of his own.
Aristophanes seems to have regarded him as the most
influential and dangerous teacher in that Sophistic
school against which his own first literary work, *The
Banqueters*, had been written. In that non-extant
comedy, he contrasted the characters of two young men,
the one Decorous, the other Dissolute: the former
educated in the old Athenian fashion, the latter on the
most approved model of the new Sophistic school. See
Nub. 537. The same idea recurs in *The Clouds*, but
worked out in a different manner. Sokrates there appears in his Hall of Contemplation, as the great Master
of Sophistry, the teacher of lessons inculcating nothing
short of the most barefaced irreligion and immorality.
The controversies arising upon this comedy cannot be
considered here. They are amply discussed in Thirlwall's and Grote's *Histories of Greece*, in K. O. Müller's

and Bernhardy's *Histories of Greek Literature*, and in Süvern's *Essay on The Clouds*. It seems absurd to suppose that *The Clouds* had any influence in determining the judicial murder of Sokrates twenty-four years afterwards. It failed to secure the first or second prize; and, although Aristophanes revised his work, and prepared a second edition, which is the drama we now possess, yet, if this was reproduced on the Athenian stage (a doubtful point), it was again unsuccessful.

§ 19. The lampoons of Aristophanes are not to be defended on ethical grounds, whether we abandon them to the stern censure of Mr Grote, or seek shelter for them in the milder appreciation of Bishop Thirlwall. It is not in the jests and sketches of *Punch*, or *Vanity Fair*, or *Figaro*, or *Kladderadatsch*, that we look for the pure abstractions of moral truth. The personalities of the Old Comedy, like its grossness, came 'ex hamaxês;' they were a part of the Bacchic licence, the wares of the ancient waggon. The men of Athens of all classes, from the statesman to the scavenger, filled the theatre twice a year for the sake of fun and frolic; and these they found, not in serious tragic verities, but (like Londoners flocking to a Christmas pantomime) in extravagant buffooneries, which, pretending to be true, set truth itself at defiance. Who can imagine for a single instant, that the outrageous calumnies heaped on Kleon or Sokrates obtained credence, or were supposed by the poet to obtain credence, with any portion of the Athenian audience? They were ingredients in the mirth of the feast, designed mainly to provoke laughter; and were in fact more amusing, in proportion as their exaggeration was more amazing. There is nothing to hinder us from believing that the same artisan, who to-day listened with greedy ear and chuckling delight to the libellous insolence of the Sausage-seller in *The Knights*, would hold up his hand to-morrow with unabated zeal for Kleon's measures in the Ekklesia. No facts in history lead us to suppose that Comedy exercised an important political influence. Nor should it be forgotten that Aristophanes caters to the amusement of his audience, not only by exaggerating in the most ridiculous manner the imputed sins and follies of others, but also by enhancing his own merits and claims, or his assumed wrongs, with ironical absurdity, thus, in fact, provoking laughter at his own expense. How racy, for instance, is the humour of the following passage in the parabasis of *The Acharnians* (643, etc.), the third comedy composed by Aristophanes, and not produced, any more than the former two, in his own name! How typical is it of the audacious irony of modern advertisers, when they bring themselves or their inventions for the first time before a gaping public with the attractive epithet 'World-renowned!'

"All the envoys conveying you tribute will come from the cities,
 desiring to gaze on
This most excellent poet who ventured to speak in the ears of
 Athenians plain justice.
And so far does the fame of his courage extend, that the Great
 King, examining lately
The Lakonian ambassadors, questioned them first, of the parties engaged in the struggle
Which was stronger in ships, and then, which of the twain
 from this poet got plenty of scolding:

> These, he said, became braver by far, and in war they would
> conquer, obtaining such counsel.
> Hence the Lakedaemonians offer you peace, and would have
> you restore them Aegina,
> Though they care not a fig for that island, not they; only
> want to win from you this poet."

The freedom with which Aristophanes ventures to ridicule and caricature the deities of Greece is explained by the same tradition of unbridled licence in the Vintage-feast, which made all things in heaven and earth subject to its drunken dominion. Dionysus himself, its patron-god, figures in *The Frogs* as a poltroon, and is scourged as a vagabond in Orcus, to the greater glory of himself and his festival. The funniest scenes in *The Birds* are those which introduce Prometheus the deserter, Herakles the gourmand, and Triballus, a barbarian god of comic coinage.

§ 20. The literary career of Aristophanes falls into three distinct periods. The first of these, commencing with *The Banqueters*, B.C. 428, and *The Babylonians* in 427, includes the first five extant comedies, ending with *The Peace*, B.C. 422; and three others not extant also belong to this period, *The Merchantmen*, *The Farmers*, and *The Proagon*. During those years the democratic constitution of Athens was in full force, and Aristophanes exercises the most unrestrained freedom of speech on political facts, principles, and persons. An interval of seven years succeeds, during which there is no record of plays composed by Aristophanes, though we can hardly suppose his genius was lying fallow through the vigorous season of manhood. Those were years of nominal peace be-

tween Athens and the Peloponnesians. But the warlike
temper was only smouldering, till the ambition of Alkibiades, who was now in competition with Nikias for the
leadership, could find a good opportunity to blow it into
flame again. An occasion at length presented itself in
the quarrels of the Sicilian states; one of which, Egesta,
solicited the aid of Athens. This the Athenians, at the
instigation of Alkibiades, and against the advice of
Nikias, undertook to give, nominally for the protection of
their allies, but really with the rash design of capturing
Syracuse, and conquering the whole island, B.C. 415.

§ 21. With this era begins the second period of our
poet's literary career. He brought out, in the name of
Philonides, a play called *Amphiaraus*, at the Lenaea;
and at the Dionysia of the city, B.C. 414, in the name of
Kallistratus he produced *The Birds*. This, the most
imaginative and captivating of his works, obtained the
second prize only, the first being awarded to *The Komastae*
of Ameipsias, the third to *The Monotropus* of Phrynichus.
The same period comprises *The Lysistrata* and *The
Thesmophoriazusae*, B.C. 411, the first *Plutus*, B.C. 408,
and *The Frogs*, B.C. 405. It was, politically speaking,
a time of revolution, struggle, and disaster domestic and
foreign, when the minds of the Athenians were tossed to
and fro with doubts, difficulties and alarms. It began
with a secret conspiracy against the democratic constitution; which, after the Sicilian calamity, was overthrown
in 411, and an oligarchy of four hundred established.
That usurpation did not long endure: but with revived
democracy calm was not restored, and, after a few years
of alternating success and defeat, Lysander's victory at

Aegospotami and his capture of Athens, B.C. 404, subjugated the city for a time to the narrower and more cruel domination of the Thirty.

§ 22. Few thoughtful minds pass through a long revolutionary time without some variation of feeling and opinion. But there is no proof that any violent change occurred in the sentiments of Aristophanes. Hostile as he was to democratic excess, and partial to the principles and habits of olden days, he shews no sympathy with the schemes of the oligarchic faction. But we cannot fail to recognise in his comedies of this middle period a certain reticence and caution, contrasting very strikingly with the outspoken audacity of his earlier works. If in *The Birds* there is any political purpose—which is a disputed question—that purpose is covert, and studiously disguised. Allusions to passing events and personal character are few, and expressed with more of irony than virulence. In *The Thesmophoriazusae* there is nothing political; in *The Frogs* next to nothing. In *The Lysistrata*, the poet gives free scope to his hatred of the war; but this he might safely do when his country had just sustained a military reverse so terrible as the destruction of its army and fleet in Sicily. And his anti-warlike sentiments are expressed with more security by being ascribed to women, and associated with a ludicrous insurrection of the Athenian and Spartan wives against marital authority. Upon the whole, then, we may say that the Muse of Aristophanes, in this middle period of her career, shews herself a much more prudential personage than during the first part of the Peloponnesian war. And well might she deport herself modestly in times when political faction had begun to arm against the foes who annoyed it, not only the fatal ballot of the tribunal, but also the secret poniard of the assassin.

§ 23. The third and last Aristophanic period contains only two extant plays, *The Ekklesiazusae*, and the second *Plutus*. They were acted some years after the expulsion of the Thirty. But though democracy was now finally restored by the victories of Thrasybulus and Konon, the wings of Comedy had been clipt in the archonship of Eukleides; personalities were restrained, and the parabasis disused. *The Plutus* indeed belongs rather to the Middle than to the Old Comedy. In *The Ekklesiazusae*, by burlesquing the Platonic theory of communism, our poet shews himself what he was from the outset, a staunch opponent of new lights in philosophy, morals, and politics. But this play, though it often sparkles with his brilliant wit, is inferior on the whole as a work of art, besides being intolerably gross. Among the comedies written by him later still, towards the close of his life, we have the names of three, *Kokalus*, *Tagenistae*, *Aiolosikon*. The last of these he is said to have left for his son Araros to produce. The dates of his other Comedies are uncertain. On that called *Géras* (Old Age) see Süvern's Essay, published at the end of his Essay on *The Clouds*.

§ 24. A literary controversy has gathered round *The Birds* as round *The Clouds*. The scope and plan of the drama are the question in dispute. Is it a purely historical allegory? Is it a philosophical allegory? Is it an allegory at all? Or is it merely a work of the imagination, a poetic *Lustspiel*, a *Midsummer Night's Dream*?

§ 25. The discussion of this question was opened about half a century ago, by the remarkable Essay of Professor Süvern, read in 1825 before the Royal Academy of Sciences at Berlin, and translated into English by Mr W. R. Hamilton in 1836. The purpose of this treatise is to shew that in *The Birds* is found a purely historical allegory, explained by the Sicilian expedition and the parties concerned in it. The design of capturing Syracuse and conquering Sicily is typified by the foundation of the Bird-city, Cloudcuckooborough. The Athenians are represented chiefly by the Birds, partly also by men. The gods signify the Lakedaemonians and their chief allies: the walling out and starving of the gods implies a blockade of Peloponnesus by Athenian fleets commanding the Mediterranean. Iris is an escaped Peloponnesian galley. The Hoopoe with his triple crest indicates the Athenian commander Lamachus. Peithetaerus is a compound of Alkibiades and Gorgias. Euelpides is both one of the 'hopeful' Athenians (see Thuk. VI. 24), and at the same time Polus of Agrigentum, the 'famulus' of Gorgias. This marvellous theory was supported by such an ingenious array of learned argument, that on its first publication it gained much assent: and the Essay may still be read with profit, even by those who do not accept its conclusions. But, as scholar after scholar assailed it with powerful reasoning, and exposed its inherent improbabilities, it lost credit; and at the present time it will hardly find a single champion left. Can it, indeed, be reasonably supposed that Aristophanes, who in B.C. 425 had written an allegorical play (*The Knights*), quite transparent in its general meaning and in its details, would produce, ten years afterwards, another allegory, not less elaborate, and yet so dark and doubtful, that no spectator could see through it at the time, no commentator interpret it subsequently, till at length, after the lapse of 2240 years, a German scholar was found capable of reading the riddle with the minutest accuracy? No! an allegorizing comic poet could never have intended to be so obscure a Sphinx, and to look so far into the future for an Oedipus.

§ 26. Another school of criticism consists of those German writers, who find in *The Birds* a philosophical or, at least, a philosophizing allegory. The foremost representative of this school is Rötscher (1827), whose work, already cited, is designed to prove that this comedy describes, as shewn in the Athenian commonwealth, the victory of subjective opinion over objective and universal truth, of headstrong self-will over the restraints of law and order. This outline is filled in with much minute detail of the parts taken by the several characters and by the chorus. A similar view is that of Kerst (*die Vögel* 1847), who extends the purpose of the poet from the narrow field of Athens to the sphere of human government and general law; while he contends at the same time that an under-current of political design runs through the play. Wieck (*Ueber die Vögel* 1852) finds in it the antithesis of tragic heroism, a comic conception of plebeian heroism, trampling down with irresistible force all law, all religion, all ideality. This notion may have been suggested to Wieck by the outbreak of Parisian communism in 1848. According to Bohtz, Aristophanes, tired of exposing individual follies, lets the Athenians see, in one allegoric picture, the effect of living in a state composed of fools and maniacs. Cloud-cuckooborough thus becomes a sort of poetic Bedlam. To this list of scholars must be added the more eminent name of Bernhardy, who, in his *Gr. Lit.* II. 989, seems to fluctuate between two views, one exhibiting in *The Birds* 'an ochlocratic commonwealth,' the other, a mere poetic phantasy. It were waste of time to scrutinize more minutely theories of this nature, which represent Teutonic rather than Hellenic thought, the mind of Hegel more than that of Aristophanes.

§ 27. K. O. Müller (*Gr. Lit.* Ch. xxviii.) says:

"The whole piece is a satire on Athenian frivolity and credulity, on that building of castles in the air, and that dreaming expectation of a life of luxury and ease, to which the Athenian people gave themselves up in the mass; but the satire is so general, there is so little of anger and bitterness, so much of fantastic humour in it, that no comedy could make a more agreeable and harmless impression."

According to this view, the Bird-city does not represent either Athens or Syracuse, and Peithetaerus does not represent Alkibiades. The play conveys indeed to the Athenians warning and instruction, but of a general kind, without special advice adapted to the political situation of the time.

§ 28. Against this description of *The Birds*, as 'a castle in the air,' Dr Köchly, Rector of the University of Zurich, strongly contends in his *Gratulationsschrift* to Boeckh (*über die Vögel des Ar.* 1857). His main argument is: that, considering the analogy of his other plays, especially of *The Acharnians*, *The Knights*, *The Wasps*, *The Peace*, *The Lysistrata*, and *The Frogs*,

Aristophanes must be understood to sympathize with those who are victorious at the end; and, in *The Birds*, these are Peithetaerus and the Bird-commonwealth. After a skilful analysis of the plot, after describing the miserable condition of Athens at the time, distracted by the bitter strife between democrats and oligarchs, infidels and bigots, Köchly says that Aristophanes had now renounced the method used in his earlier works, of representing these opposite tendencies in concrete embodiments; that he had abandoned his youthful dream of recurring to an 'Old-Athens,' and was now disposed to recommend the transition to a 'New-Athens,' the type of which he places in the free realm of air, among its denizens, the genial Birds. From this 'New-Athens' degenerate evils of every kind, political and religious, must be removed; religion must be preserved, but in subordination to the State; democracy must be maintained, but a Periklean democracy, under a supreme leader. Nor does he shrink from supposing that the leader so recommended is Alkibiades, though then placed under capital accusation, if not already known to be a fugitive and a proscribed exile. In support of this opinion Köchly appeals to the favour a second time shewn to the same Alkibiades, during his later exile, in *The Frogs*, where, when Euripides and Aeschylus are desired by Dionysus to give their opinions about the banished leader, the reply of Aeschylus, who represents the mind of Aristophanes, is this:

"Rear not within the state a lion's cub:
But, being reared, submit ye to his ways."

§ 29. Dr Köchly found a courteous opponent in

his friend and colleague, Professor Vögelin, who, in a letter addressed to him in 1858, advocates an opinion, that the scope of *The Birds* is poetical only, not political in any special manner. He leans therefore to the view originally taken by Aug. W. Schlegel in his *Lectures on Dramatic Literature*, and virtually adopted by Droysen, by the brothers Karl and Theodor Kock, and other scholars. According to this view the comedy is in its conception a fantastic dream, a *Lustspiel*, or (to borrow the title of Mr Courthope's genial work) a *Paradise of Birds*. The Muse of Aristophanes flies from an old city full of trouble and discomfort to a new colony of ease and enjoyment; and the sentiment is very much that of Schiller's secular ode,—

"Freiheit ist nur in dem Reich der Träume,
Und das Schöne blüht nur im Gesang."

§ 30. Another and not insignificant shade of opinion remains to be noticed. In the judgment of some scholars the religion of the Athenians and of Hellas generally is the central subject of *The Birds*. Binaut's idea, that the abolition of the old faith and the reception of new formulas is suggested by Aristophanes, may indeed be set aside as extravagant and untenable. Seeger regards the piece as a humorous criticism of the Hellenic national religion. This description is open to the charge of one-sidedness; but perhaps it draws attention to a really important feature of the poet's design in composing this play. See § 46-8.

§ 31. In order to mediate, if possible, between these various and conflicting views, it will be convenient, at this point, to sketch briefly the political state of

Athens at the moment when *The Birds* was acted : and then to consider the plot and management of the drama itself, with special notice of those passages which indicate any feelings of the poet respecting the characters, events and controversies of the time.

§ 32. When the Sicilian expedition was voted B.C. 415, there were in Athens three political parties. The democratic majority, partisans of progress and of war, who had formerly supported Kleon, were now led by the daring, able, and unprincipled Alkibiades, who, born of high family and possessing great wealth, flattered the popular ambition to serve his own, and sought personal aggrandizement in the aggrandizement of his country. A smaller but not inconsiderable body of citizens, moderate in political feeling, were generally guided by the advice of Nikias, whose pacific and conservative character was liable to the dangerous faults of indolence and superstition. Behind these parties lay in the shade a third, the oligarchic faction, not large in numbers, and afraid to avow itself, but formidable from its organization, which was conducted by secret societies or clubs, called Hetaeries (hetaireiai). The members of these societies were bound by oath to support each other mutually in lawsuits and candidature for office, and to propagate their common political objects at the risk of property and life. The partisans of Nikias disliked the character and dreaded the policy of Alkibiades : the oligarchic clubbists went farther still ; they hated him personally, as the French aristocrats in 1789 hated Lafayette, considering him a deserter from his order, and one who fostered democratic influence as the basis of a virtual tyranny for himself. Among the leaders of these Hetaeries in 415 were, Andokides, son of Leogoras, a young and wealthy Eupatrid, Peisander (Peisandrus) of Acharnae, a cowardly intriguer, who afterwards became a traitor, Charikles, in later years one of the Thirty, and the orator Antiphon, son of the sophist Sophilus. Of these, Antiphon alone had been hitherto bold enough to oppose Alkibiades in public. Nor was it in these political parties only that Alkibiades had enemies at work against him. Many of the small fry in the Ekklesia, Kleonymus, Androkles, and others, envied his popularity, and resented the stings of his scornful eloquence. The priests, with Lampon and Diopeithes at their head, abhorred the freethinker, whose mockeries of religion impaired their influence, and might tend to diminish their profits. The comic stage was enlisted in the same cause. Eupolis probably exhibited at the Dionysia of the city, in March 415, his comedy called *The Baptae*, in which the licentious revels and nocturnal profanities of Alkibiades and his boon companions were held up to public indignation. This attack is said to have irritated Alkibiades, but it did not avail to shake his influence.

§ 33. The expedition to Sicily had been voted (§ 20), and the preparation of the armament was proceeding. The opponents of the scheme had called in the aid of superstition to prevent its execution, but without success. Deterring oracles had been reported from the shrine of Ammon. Ravens had stolen the fruit from the golden palm-tree at Delphi. The women celebrating the festival of Adonis were said to have heard sounds of lamentation issuing from the rafters. Sokrates, it was rumoured, had been warned by his daemon of impending failure. The mathematician Meton had set his house on fire, either to escape service himself as a lunatic, or to detain his son at home. All in vain. The popular will was paramount: and the armada continued its preparation, when a fact occurred which startled Athens, and led to the most momentous consequences. This was the mutilation of the Hermae, justly called by Mr Grote 'one of the most extraordinary events in all Grecian history.' These Hermae, or half-statues of the god Hermes, are described by the same historian as 'blocks of marble about the size of the human figure.' He goes on to say of them:

"The upper part was cut into a head, face, neck, and bust; the lower part was left as a quadrangular pillar, broad at the base, without arms, body, or legs. They were distributed in great numbers throughout Athens, and always in the most conspicuous situations; standing beside the outer doors of private houses as well as of temples—near the most frequented porticoes—at the intersection of cross-ways—in the public agora. They were thus present to the eyes of every Athenian in all his acts of intercommunion, either for business or pleasure, with his fellow-citizens. The religious feeling of the Greeks considered the god to be planted or domiciliated where his statue stood, so that the companionship, sympathy, and guardianship of Hermes became associated with most of the manifestations of conjunct life at Athens, political, social, commercial, or gymnastic. Moreover, the quadrangular fashion of these statues, employed occasionally for other gods besides Hermes, was a most ancient relic handed down from the primitive rudeness of Pelasgian workmanship; and was popular in Arcadia, as well as peculiarly frequent in Athens."

On the morning of the 11th of May, B.C. 415, all these Hermae were found to have been mutilated by unknown hands. The characteristic features of each had been destroyed, and nothing left but a rude mass of stone. One Hermes only had been spared, if the account given by Andokides may be trusted; and that stood near the house of his father Leogoras.

§ 34. The effect produced by so daring a sacrilege on the population of what Sophokles (*Oed. Col.* 260) calls the most god-revering of cities, could not fail to be tremendous: and it is ably depicted as such by Grote, in the passage which follows the last citation. Horror, alarm, confusion, suspicion were widely felt, and everywhere displayed; for those who were in the secret counterfeited these emotions, and strove to propagate them. Historians are agreed, for the most part, that the crime was conceived and executed with a view to depopularize and destroy Alkibiades: and the secrecy of its execution points to the oligarchic hetaeries as the contrivers and agents. Their plan was to fanaticize the popular mind by this sacrilege, and, when inquisition was made, to extend the inquiry to all offences against religion, by which means they could not fail to inculpate Alkibiades. In this course they might calculate with full assurance on the aid of the priests, headed by the same Diopeithes who, seventeen years before, under the administration of Perikles, had inspired and conducted the measures against the philosopher Anaxagoras, which compelled him to fly from Athens. Unsuccessful in their former efforts, the clubbists were resolved, by one grand *coup*, to succeed now. And succeed they did in their main object, the ruin of their hated rival; but with him they ruined the Sicilian enterprise, they ruined their country, and in the long run, by a righteous retribution, they ruined themselves and their party.

§ 35. The Council of 500 met, and summoned a special Ekklesia, which voted a Commission of Inquiry. Among the chief inquisitors were Peisander and Charikles, who were not improbably in the secret of the plot. A reward of 10,000 drachmas (nearly £400) was offered for information: but none as yet came in. A further reward of 1000 drachmas was then proposed, on the motion of Kleonymus, for all information respecting acts committed in violation of religious worship. Still several weeks passed without any denunciation. At length, on the very day when the strategi (Nikias, Lamachus and Alkibiades) were to report the completion of the armament, and receive their final orders from the people, one Pythonikus, an agent of the conspirators, mounted the *bema*, and warned the citizens of the danger incurred by sending as commander of the fleet a violator of the highest religious sanctities. Alkibiades, he said, had profaned religion by a mock celebration of the Eleusinian mysteries in the house of Polytion, and in the company of other profligate young men. A slave Andromachus was brought forward to establish this charge by his evidence: and Pythonikus went on to denounce Alkibiades as implicated in the mutilation of the Hermae; a gross and manifest calumny. Whether for this reason or for others, the accusation did not gain credence. Androkles renewed and extended the charges in another Assembly, but the resolute denial of Alkibiades was received with applause. Hereupon the conspirators, affecting moderation, proposed to withdraw them for the time, and to defer the inquiry concerning the mysteries till the return of Alkibiades. Against this course he himself protested strongly, demanding an immediate trial, a full acquittal or a capital condemnation. His friends do not seem to have discerned as clearly as he did the wisdom of insisting on this demand. He was not adequately supported; and his enemies so far succeeded as to send him to Sicily without a previous trial and acquittal. This was in July, 415.

§ 36. After the departure of the fleet, the inquisition was continued on all the matters of charge. And now information poured in: first from one Teukrus, a resident alien (metoikos); then from a woman named Agariste, and from Lydus a slave. These inculpated numerous persons, of whom many fled, others were imprisoned. Afterwards one Diokleides appeared with a tale of 300 conspirators, of whom he said he had seen 42 assembled in the street on the night of the mutilation of the Hermae, and had been enabled by the moonlight to discern their faces. He specified two senators, with many more persons, among whom were Andokides and his father Leogoras, with several of their kinsmen. The senators, threatened with torture, fled, the rest were thrown into prison. And now Andokides, to save his father and kinsfolk (as he alleges in his speech 'on the Mysteries' many years later) was induced, after promise of indemnity, to make a confession, implicating among the Hermokopidae one Euphiletus, and many others, as principals, and himself as a tacit accomplice, who had not taken part in the act, being confined to the house by an accident: for proof of which he referred to the unmutilated state of the Hermes adjoining his father's house. The prisoners accused by Andokides were executed. Those who had fled were condemned in their absence and became disfranchised (atimoi). This confession led to a re-examination of the tale of Diokleides, which was now disproved; and he, admitting his falsehood, was put to death. To what extent Andokides spoke the truth, was never known[1]. We may guess that what he did tell was not far from fact, but that he could have told much more, if he had chosen. All but four of those whom he inculpated had been denounced already by Teukrus, among them Euphiletus. The four scapegoats were perhaps sacrificed to give a colour of truth to his narrative: but we have no clue to shew the reason why they were selected. As they escaped and became exiles, it is probable they had warning beforehand. These events are narrated by Mr Grote with more fulness of detail than our present purpose needs.

[1] The whole tenour of this affair leads to the conjecture, that the slaves and Agariste were witnesses prepared by the Hetaeries in their own interest against Alkibiades, but that Teukrus and Diokleides were unlooked for and unwelcome interlopers, whose appearance had the effect of "hoisting the oligarchic engineers with their own petard." Teukrus, who had retired to Megara, and did not return and testify till he got a promise of safety, was probably an agent betraying his employers for the sake of gain, and care was taken that his share of gain should be a very small one. Diokleides, there is no room to doubt, was a needy speculator making a bold stroke for a fortune; a shrewd man, we may guess, who knew his Athens, its families, and parties, pretty well; who had waited and watched, and drawn his conclusions more or less sagaciously, and with more or less correctness. He was able to put forward a plausible list of 300 conspirators, and from these to make a plausible selection of the 42, whom

§ 37. The charges of impiety were renewed against Alkibiades in his absence. And so many acts of this kind were now imputed, that his enemies found it an easy matter to obtain a decree of accusation against him, and of recall to answer the charge in person. His impeachment (eisangelia) before the Council of 500 was moved by Thessalus son of Kimon, one of the oligarchic party, and seconded by the democratic orator Androkles. The motion being accepted, the state-galley Salaminia was despatched to summon him home: the trierarch being ordered not to seize his person, but to allow him to sail to Athens in his own galley. The Salaminia found the Athenian fleet at Katana, in Sicily. Alkibiades obeyed the summons, but on the homeward voyage he escaped from Thurii in Italy, and afterwards, being received at Sparta, he traitorously betrayed the plans of Athens, and advised the Lakedaemonians to assist the Syracusans, invade Attica and fortify Dekeleia. These counsels were adopted with success.

§ 38. On the return of the Salaminia to Athens without Alkibiades, he was condemned to death as a traitor *par contumace*, his property was confiscated, and a solemn curse was pronounced upon him by the

he had seen, as he said, by moonlight during the momentous night. The unmutilated Hermes would, for one thing, signalize to him the young Andokides, about whom he would naturally enquire and gather more. And, having fixed on this young man, he thought it a safe course to include his father Leogoras and many of his kindred. But here the informer too 'hoisted' himself. He drove to confession a real conspirator, whose tale, founded on a knowledge of facts, soon destroyed the guess-work fabric of Diokleides, and consigned to the executioner a perjured villain, who a short while before had been crowned amidst popular applause, escorted to the Prytaneum, and feasted there.

priests. E. Curtius describes in the following passage of his History (Prof. Ward's *Translation*, III. 341) the miserable state of Athenian society resulting from the affair of the Hermokopidae and the intrigues which followed it.

"This was the first victory achieved by party intrigues at Athens over the state and its interests; the end of a struggle which had for months agitated the community, and brought into play all the decomposing elements existing in it: hatred and passion, impudent audacity and hypocrisy, superstitious terror and frivolous insolence. It was a victory of the revolution over law and usage; and therefore society had not only most heavily suffered under it externally in the shape of banishments, confiscations, and capital sentences, but had also been affected in its innermost life by the consequences resulting from this victory; the sense of right and wrong was blunted, and the voice of morality drowned. Day after day the citizens had seen the most sacred ties disregarded, accused persons sacrificing those who had become their bail, and witnesses unblushingly uttering false testimony. Things had come to such a pass, that a Dioclides was crowned with the wealth bestowed upon public benefactors, and conducted in the chariot of honour to banquet in the Prytaneum; although, even before he was unmasked, he had shown himself to be a man who let it depend entirely on the question of pecuniary profit, whether he should speak or remain silent. The sur-excited minds of the populace were no longer to be satisfied with ordinary trials; in feverish excitement they followed the windings of a criminal justice working in the dark, in favour of which they became accustomed to sacrifice the enjoyment of the most important of civic rights. Accusation and condemnation seemed to be identical. Accordingly, by far the greater number of trials dealt with absent persons. The patrimony of ancient families was sold into strange hands; while the large number of fugitives could not but serve to disclose, to the enemies lying in wait outside, the actual condition of Attic society. Subsequently, indeed, most of the exiles were reinstated in their property, but the ancient evils continued to exercise their effects; a general feeling of mistrust and insecurity remained; and public confidence was permanently weakened by the fact, that, notwithstanding all the enquiries instituted, the mutilation of the Hermæ remained for all time an unsolved enigma to the Athenians."

§ 39. Such, then, was the sad condition of things at Athens, when Aristophanes produced *The Birds*, and his rivals their several plays, at the Dionysia of the city in March 414. We must suppose *The Birds* to have been finished as a literary work at least two months earlier, for the theatrical preparations and the teaching of the chorus and actors would require some such interval. As we do not know when the Salaminia reached the Peiraeus on its return, it is impossible to say whether Aristophanes was acquainted with the escape of Alkibiades at the time he finished his work: but there is no reason to suppose that the news of his treason at Sparta had arrived.

§ 40. Curtius assumes (p. 343) that the comedies which then competed were restrained in their composition by a law said to have emanated from the verbose demagogue Syrakosius, forbidding personal ridicule. This rests upon the authority of a Scholiast on *Av.* 1297, who cites a passage from *The Monotropus* of Phrynichus, inveighing against Syrakosius for taking from him the power of ridiculing whom he chose. It seems impossible to believe that at this era such a law had been carried at all, or that, if carried for a time, it was not now repealed; for, had it really been in force, how was Aristophanes able to introduce by name Syrakosius himself as having the nickname Magpie, or Peisander as a spiritless dastard, besides many other living characters? and how could he bring Meton on the stage in person?

§ 41. Let us now take a rapid survey of the plot of *The Birds*, noting more especially those points which may help us to estimate the poet's purpose in writing it.

The scene is a rocky wilderness, on which enter two Athenians, with slaves and baggage. One of these is Peithetaerus (Winfriend), an inventive genius, the other, Euelpides (Hopeful), a chattering jocular cit, with something in him of Sancho Panza, and a spice of Mark Tapley. Peithetaerus carries a crow in his left hand, Euelpides a jackdaw or jay; prophetic birds, which act as guides to the two travellers, who, *sick of litigation, worry, and expense, are migrating from Athens in search of a less troublesome abode.* Such a city they hope to find by the aid of the Hoopoe, formerly Tereus, allied by marriage to Pandion, a mythic king of Athens. With the help of their birds, they reach his residence, and obtain an interview. 'Of what country are you?' says the Hoopoe. '*Whence the gallant triremes*,' replies Euelpides. '*Are you Heliasts?*'—'*No! Heliast-haters: we seek a snug city.*'—'A greater than Athens?'—'No, but *a more comfortable one.*'—'You want an aristocracy.'—'Not at all: *I abhor Aristokrates.*'—'Well,' says the Hoopoe, 'I know such a city on the Red Sea.'—'*No sea-side place for us, where the Salaminia may come and arrest us.* But we should like to hear about the bird-life, what sort of thing it is.'—'Pleasant enough.' And now Peithetaerus, who has been wrapt in silent meditation, breaks in with the announcement of a plan for aggrandizing the Birds, *by building a city between earth and heaven, which shall intercept the savour of sacrifices, and wear the gods to death with Melian famine, compelling them to pay*

d

tribute, and surrender their dominion to the Birds. The Hoopoe, charmed with the idea, agrees to summon the Birds to a conference, in which Peithetaerus shall expound his scheme. His nightingale-wife Prokne is called out of the brake, and the two sing their pibroch of summons to the Birdtribe. It is answered first by the appearance of four peculiar birds (see v. 285), and then by the 24 who enter the orchestra and form the Chorus of the play (v. 312—322). Horrified at the sight of men, their natural enemies, their first impulse is to destroy the two Athenians, who, armed with their cooking utensils, stand on the defensive. At last the Hoopoe succeeds in cooling their wrath; and they consent to hear the exposition of Peithetaerus. He, by a series of comic instances, and by dint of a comic logic, proves to their satisfaction that *Birds were the deities originally worshipped by mankind.* 'And how are we to recover our lost dominion?' they ask in the eagerness of excited ambition. Peithetaerus develops his plan of a new Bird-city; and removes one by one the difficulties suggested. His views are accepted with enthusiasm; a vote of confidence is passed, *the Birds intreating Peithetaerus to march along with them against the gods with just, sincere, religious heart.* The Hoopoe introduces the Nightingale to his guests, enters with them into his dwelling, and does not again appear, the conduct of the Bird-nation being now left to Peithetaerus. The Chorus chant the Parabasis, which, *after a cosmogony, shewing the Birds to be more ancient than the Gods*, offers, in the epirrhema, impunity for crime as a temptation to settle in Birdland, and, in the antepirrhema, recounts various

INTRODUCTION.

advantages gained by the possession of wings. The two Athenians, changed into birds by eating a magic root, rejoin the Chorus, and, after mutual banter, adopt for the new city the title of Cloudcuckooborough (Nephelokokkygia). Euelpides is then despatched to overlook the builders, and does not reappear. Peithetaerus fetches a priest to pray and perform sacrifice, while the Birds chant a Chorikon. *The priest recites a litany, in which Birdnames are mingled in ridiculous confusion with those of the ancient deities. After which, because he had brought a lean goat for sacrifice, he is dismissed with contumely.* Emigrants from the old world apply for admission to the new city; a begging poet, *a cheating soothsayer*, the geometer Meton, an official inspector, and a vendor of plebiscites or decrees. The poet gets a dole of clothing; the rest are packed off with insults and stripes. The Chorus then sing a second imperfect Parabasis; in the epirrhema of which *a reward is offered to any one who shall kill the atheist Diagoras of Melos, or any of the dead tyrants.* Tidings come to Peithetaerus of the completion of the new city, which is ludicrously described. *Iris, the messenger of the gods, who had been despatched to require from men the usual sacrifices, is now intercepted by the Bird-scouts and brought before Peithetaerus, who sends her back to heaven with scoffs and threats.* A herald from earth relates the enthusiasm which is inspired at Athens by the foundation of the Bird-city. Crowds, he says, are on their way to demand wings. Peithetaerus, with his slaves, prepares a supply of these. The first candidate is a young man who wants to get rid of his father.

Peithetaerus dissuades him from this purpose, supplies him with wings, a spur and a crest, and sends him to fight his country's battles in Thrace. The dithyrambic poet Kinesias wants wings for his cloudy excursions. He only gets a whipping. A professed informer appears, who desires wings to fly to and from the islands in pursuit of his dishonest business. He is still more severely scourged and dismissed. A Stasimon follows, shewing up the poltroon Kleonymus and the cloak-robber Orestes. *Then enters Prometheus as a deserter from heaven, hidden under a sunshade or umbrella. He tells Peithetaerus that the gods are reduced to starvation, and are sending an embassy to treat for peace. He advises that the only terms accepted be, that the sceptre shall be restored to the Birds, and Royalty, the all-powerful handmaid of Zeus, be given to Peithetaerus in marriage.* The next Stasimon sketches Sokrates the spirit-raiser, Peisander his spiritless visitor, and Chaerephon his strong-spirited famulus. *Then appear the three divine ambassadors, Poseidon the courtier, Herakles the glutton, and Triballus the barbarian.* Peithetaerus, who is cooking a repast, of which the chief dish consists of *birds put to death for insurrection against the democratic birds*, gains the support of Herakles by the savour of dainties, and other tempting promises. Herakles wins over Triballus, and, Poseidon being thus outvoted, the demands of Peithetaerus are conceded. He proceeds to heaven with the three ambassadors to receive his bride. The following Stasimon lampoons the Sophists, especially Gorgias and Philippus, as ventriloquists, that is, men who fill their bellies by the use of their tongues.

A messenger announces the approach of the bridal pair. *Peithetaerus, who wields the thunderbolts of Zeus, descends with Royalty from a chariot* amidst the acclamations of the Birds; the nuptial procession is formed, and marches forth to the sound of exulting music.

§ 42. After considering this outline of the plot, a few questions may be usefully asked and answered. (1) Was it the purpose of Aristophanes, by the Birds to represent the Athenians, and by the foundation of Cloud-cuckooborough the Sicilian expedition? To answer in the affirmative would be nearly the same thing as to accept Süvern's allegorical theory, which has been already dismissed. The whole tenour of the play shews that the Birds are distinct from the Athenians, and rather placed in contrast with them than as representative of them. The two emigrants have quitted Athens as an uncomfortable residence. After rejecting several abodes suggested to them by the Hoopoe, they find that Bird-life itself is not unpleasant (v. 164 &c.), and Peithetaerus develops a plan for improving the condition of the Birds. This leads to various applications from Athenians (each of whom typifies some class disliked by Aristophanes), first, to be admitted as colonists (vv. 958—1126); next, to obtain wings (vv. 1419—1557). All these are disapproved, and sent back to Athens. Thus the distinction between the two localities and their several inhabitants is studiously maintained. And this general fact is in no degree weakened by the circumstance, that analogies are often exhibited between Athens and Birdland, Athenians and Birds. All this belongs to the humour of the piece, and to that form of joking by surprise, which is so large an ingredient in comic wit. See vv. 319. 367. 793—808. 875—880. 910. 932. 1492. 1543—47, &c. The Athenian audience were thus indulged with frequent opportunities of laughing at their own expense; a pleasure, no doubt, as heartily enjoyed by them, as it would be by an English audience now.

§ 43. If the Birds are not types of the Athenians, we may dismiss with a simple negative the further inquiry, whether the Bird-city and its foundation represent the Sicilian enterprise. (2) But other questions which may be raised are these: did Aristophanes in the character of Peithetaerus intend to shadow forth Alkibiades? and further, did he mean to recommend (as Köchly thinks), that the sole leadership, either of the state or of the military force, should be entrusted to Alkibiades? It cannot be denied, that between the character of Peithetaerus and that of Alkibiades there are some striking analogies. Both are dissolute: both contemners of the popular religion: both eloquent reasoners: both persuaders of men: both are ambitious, bold and able schemers. It were hazardous, therefore, to say with positive assurance, that the image of Alkibiades was not present to the poet's mind, when he drew the character of Peithetaerus. But it may fairly be stated as improbable, that he designed to *impersonate* Alkibiades in that character, and to place him distinctly before the public eye as, in *The Knights*, he had placed Kleon, Nikias, Demosthenes, and the Demus of Athens itself. It may perhaps be said, with all but absolute assurance, that he had not this purpose; for no repre-

INTRODUCTION.

sentation of a similar kind appears in any other of his works. And did Aristophanes mean to recommend Alkibiades as leader of the state or as sole 'strategus'? Such a recommendation Köchly infers, partly from the final success of Peithetaerus, and from his obtaining 'Royalty,' 'the sceptre,' and 'the thunder of Zeus': partly from the passage (vv. 658—669), where the Birds say to Peithetaerus:

"Your guidance will I nevermore forsake unto the end."

  *   *   *   *   *   *   *

"All the work, where strength is needed, be to us assign'd,
While to you shall be committed all requiring mind."

He might have added to his evidence the Hoopoe's words, which next follow (v. 670—1):

"Now, let me tell you, there's no further time
To nod and shilly-shally, Nikias-like;
But something must be done forthwith."

It is difficult to meet Köchly's inference with a decided negative. Can it be said with certainty, that, when Aristophanes composed *The Birds*, the advantage in government or in war of single direction by a powerful mind did not enter into his thoughts? He may have written with this feeling; and again the image of the ablest Athenian may have floated before him, in contrast with the indecisive caution of Nikias and the brainless valour of Lamachus. But we may say, with not less absolute assurance than before: when the play was acted, Aristophanes could not wish the Athenian public to suppose that he meant to recommend a condemned exile as leader of the state or as head of the army.

§ 44. Are we then to fall back upon the mere *Lustspiel* theory? Are we to be content with saying, in the words of A. W. Schlegel: "The Comedy of *The Birds* sparkles with the boldest and richest imagination in the province of the fantastically marvellous; it is a merry buoyant creation, bright with the gayest plumage: ...... it is a piece of the most harmless buffoonery, which has a touch at everything, gods as well as men, but without anywhere pressing towards any particular object"? Or are we to agree with Mr Symonds when he argues (*Greek Poets*, p. 260) that Aristophanes ridicules idle ambition generally, and the Sicilian enterprise in particular?

"There is no doubt" (he says) "but that Aristophanes intended in *The Birds* to ridicule the ambition of the Athenians and their inveterate gullibility. Peithetaerus and Euelpides represent in comic caricature the projectors, agitators, schemers, flatterers, who, led by Alcibiades, had imposed upon the excitable vanity of the nation. Cloudcuckootown is any castle in the air, or South Sea Bubble, which might take the fancy of the Athenian mob. But it is also more especially the project of western dominion connected with their scheme of Sicilian conquest. Aristophanes has treated his theme so poetically and largely that the interest of *The Birds* is not, like that of *The Wasps* or *The Knights*, almost wholly confined to the Athens of his day. It transcends those limitations of place and time, and is the everlasting allegory of foolish schemes and flimsy ambition. A modern dramatist—Ben Jonson or Molière for instance, perhaps even Shakspere—could hardly have refrained from ending the allegory with some piece of poetical justice. We should have seen Peithetaerus disgraced and Cloudcuckootown resolved into 'such stuff as dreams are made of.' But this is not the art of Aristophanes. He brings Peithetaerus to a successful catastrophe, and ends his Comedy with marriage songs of triumph. Yet none the less pointed is the satire. The unreality of the vision is carefully maintained, and Peithetaerus walking home with Basileia for his bride, like some new sun-eclipsing star, seems to wink and strut and shrug his shoulders, conscious of the Titanic sham."

45. Neither of these views represents our conception of *The Birds*. We cannot think, with Schlegel, that this play—that any play of Aristophanes—is so mere a sport of the poetic fancy, so totally devoid of ulterior and specific design. Nor can we believe, with Mr Symonds, that the poet would, in 414, desire to assail with unsparing ridicule an enterprise upon which the Athenian people had *already* risked almost their whole material strength, in which they had invested their largest and fondest hopes. And how does this idea harmonize with that which may be called the keynote of the comedy, the reason assigned by the emigrants for leaving Athens (vv. 39—51), that they want to find a residence free from litigation, its troubles, and its unpleasant consequences? We think it probable, that the particular purpose of *The Birds* will be most truly and fully seen, if in the first place we regard this keynote attentively, as interpreted by the political events, feelings, and conditions of the time; and if in the next place, running our eye through the play, we observe how large a space in it is occupied with comic ridicule of the Hellenic deities and their priesthood.

§ 46. The gloom and terror which then prevailed at Athens, with the causes which produced them, have been sufficiently described already. The displeasure they would excite in the mind of Aristophanes might be conjectured from the character and tendencies of the man himself, and from many passages in his former plays: but these feelings are but thinly disguised, if disguised at all, in the comedy of *The Birds* itself. Besides the crucial passage above cited, we find in v. 116, vv. 154—5, vv. 1145—6, and in the characters of the Plebiscite-vendor, the Informer, Kleonymus, Peisander, indication sufficient of the disgust with which our poet viewed the suspicion and terrorism which then afflicted Athens. But whence came this terrorism, this suspicion? From an insane fanaticism. Aristophanes discerned clearly enough the cause of the mischief; and it is against this cause, in our opinion, that he contends in *The Birds*: contends, not with an open declaration of his polemical purpose, but by using the well-known and recognized comic licence of laughing at the gods, on whose part so much furious zeal had been roused, in whose name so many unjust prosecutions had been instituted, so many cruel sentences passed. This, in short, we venture to regard as the political characteristic of *The Birds*: it is meant to be *an antidote to the religious fanaticism which was the bane of Athens at that time.* If the reader will turn to the following passages in the translation, he will find that, out of 1865 lines, at least 550 are occupied with ridicule of the gods and their priesthood, and with details of their humiliation and defeat. See vv. 493. 505. 541—7. 585—617. 641—669. 720—778. 870—879. 916—956. 1019—1054. 1250—1347, 1586—1865. But amidst this general flouting of the deities, it may be noticed that one god, and he a very vulnerable one, escapes. This is Hermes, the deity whom, in *The Peace*, Aristophanes had signally caricatured. In *The Birds*, Iris, the feminine messenger of

INTRODUCTION. lix

heaven, has to bear the brunt of comic persiflage. Is it not probable, that the poet shrank from recalling to the minds of the audience that god to whose images so gross an affront had been lately offered, arousing such a storm of popular wrath? He would not run the risk of laughing to scorn a deity whose wrongs were so fresh in the public mind. But he could venture to relax the clenched teeth and unknit the frowning brows of his audience by reminding them, that to banter the Olympians generally was a privilege allowed at the Dionysiac festivals[1].

§ 47. Since allusion has been made to *The Peace*, it is not out of place to say that, as in some respects introducing and illustrating *The Birds*, this comedy may be read with interest and advantage. The two stand next to each other in the series of Aristophanic plays, and, though seven years intervene between them, there is no record of any work of our poet composed in that interval. It seems highly probable that the general idea of the Birds, of Bird-life and a Bird-city, as the ground-work of a comedy, had been revolved in the mind of Aristophanes for some years before he finally executed the design; and it is just possible that it may have grown out of his own language in *The Peace*, where the daughter of Trygaeus says to her father, as, mounted on his beetle, he is about to take flight through the air, v. 114:

"O father! O father! and is it then true
That to home and to us you are bidding adieu,
That you purpose to fly with the birds through the heavens,
And to rush in your windy career—to the ravens?"

[1] See Appendix C, Note XI.

If this conjecture be near the truth, we may well suppose that Aristophanes would defer the constitution of his plot, so far as it concerned Athenian events and characters, till the time drew near when he meant to produce it on the stage. And, when the sad troubles of the spring and summer of 415 had embittered and afflicted the Athenian mind, he would seek to divert his townsmen from their gloom, and to deal, from behind his comic shield, a smart slap in the face to Lampon, Diopeithes and the whole confederacy of priests, soothsayers, and oligarchs. And this Aristophanes could dare to do, because he was a great poet of a people thus described by Geppert (*Die Altgriechische Bühne*, p. 278):

"The Greeks denied nothing to their artist. They willingly delivered up to him all and everything, to fashion as he chose. To the comic poet they surrendered their deities, their political institutions, their public and private life, their social relations, even their own persons: all they required in return was, that he should produce a work worthy of such a god as Dionysus. And their poets have used the gift in a way which excites amazement. A creative power of humour and wit, which flung aside all fetters, has given birth to works of art, such as no time can rival. They are caricatures indeed, but in the largest style: they are parodies, but of a kind in which the spirit of the age seizes the mask, and plays its own comedy. The Demus of Athens, the very Genus of Hellas, is the acting character in these inspired outbursts of comic scorn; nay, it is also the suffering character, for it parodies itself. So was it with the Greeks. Yes, there has been a people proud enough to obey no laws but those of its own making; great enough to laugh at its own follies: a vigorous, youthful people, able to think and feel, as no nation of the earth has since their times thought and felt."

§ 48. The 'Skenê' of the Greek theatre was a permanent façade of stone, with two stories, having doors, windows, balconies, &c. capable of being modified by pictorial hangings so as to suit each particular drama. In the first scene of this play, and till near its close, the picture exhibited is that of rock and wood, without any building; but the Hoopoe's dwelling (according to Schönborn) is in an upper balcony; and the same scholar imagines that the two Athenians, when assailed by the Birds, establish their redoubt in another balcony (?). Rocks and bushes of painted wood or wickerwork must have been also used on the stage, with concealed steps, as indicated by the action of the characters in the Prologos. In tragedy five entrances are usual; a central door in the Skenê, with two others, between which it stands equidistant; also a door on each side of the stage. Such entrances are to be supposed in this play: but Schönborn seems to make no use of the right side entrance, unless he brings the four birds through it. The Athenians enter the stage from the left side, which represents the way to Hellas; and all the subsequent human characters, except the Priest (whom Aristophanes considers, according to Schönborn, an ubiquitous sort of creature) make their entrance and exit by this route. The central door is a rock, which opens for the Runner-bird and the Hoopoe. The left-centre leads to the nightingale's retreat; the right-centre is at first used by the Hoopoe to call the Birds, but afterwards it becomes the road to and from the new city. The first four birds come on the stage, in Schönborn's view (see Appendix C. Note III); but whether by the right side, or the right back entrance, he does not say: perhaps they enter by one and retire by the other. Peithetaerus, Hoopoe, &c. retire (v. 706) through the central door; and the Athenians, after the Parabasis, come out through it again. Peithetaerus uses it to fetch the Priest, who again retires through it. Euelpides goes to the works (v. 896) by the right back entrance, through which all the Messengers come and go; but the Herald comes from the left side and retires through the centre. Iris appears by the aid of machinery on the ledge of a balcony over the right back entrance, and is probably carried away on the right side again. The stealthy Prometheus, according to Schönborn's probable conjecture, comes in through the little-used left back entrance: but no good reason is given for bringing in the three divine envoys from the left side. The right side is a more probable entrance for them. On the supposed change of scene before their arrival, see foot-note on v. 1656 (1565). If the scene was changed, the 'parapetasma' (curtain) had been raised during the operation, and, on its dropping, the alcove kitchen was seen in the back centre, and Peithetaerus with slaves within it, when the gods come on. At the end of this scene, all retire through this alcove. After the speech of the third Messenger, Peithetaerus and Basileia, splendidly apparelled (the former also carrying mimic thunderbolts of Zeus), are wafted by a machine from the right side, and descend in it slowly to the stage, while they are greeted by the songs of the chorus and by mute attendants. After returning thanks and inviting the chorus to the marriage, the bridal pair retire in rhythmical step through the central door, amidst the loud acclaim of the chorus and its musicians. And so this comedy concludes. On the machinery by which the sights, sounds, and transitions of the Greek drama were effected, and on the masks, dresses, and decorations, see *Theatre of the Greeks*, Book III, ch. I. p. 210, &c. (Ed. 7.)

§ 49. The disappearance from the action of the play, first of the Hoopoe, at v. 706 (675), afterwards of Euelpides at v. 897 (846), is due to the circumstance that three actors only were employed in the dialogue parts of a Greek drama, and that the two actors who severally represented the Hoopoe and Euelpides were required to take other parts. These three actors were called respectively 'protagonistes,' 'deuteragonistes,' and 'tritagonistes.' In *The Birds* the DRAMATIS PERSONAE were probably distributed as follows:

Protagonistes.	*Deuteragonistes.*	*Tritagonistes.*
Peithetaerus.	Euelpides.	Runnerbird.
	Poet.	Hoopoe.
	Meton.	Priest.
	Plebiscite-vendor.	Soothsayer.
	Iris.	Inspector.
	Kinesias.	First Messenger.
	Prometheus.	Second Messenger.
	Herakles.	Herald.
		Parricide.
		Informer.
		Poseidon.
		Third Messenger.

Any number of 'mute persons' might be employed, as in this play the nightingale and raven (flutists), the slaves, cooks, &c. The Triballian god is an exceptional character. He appears on the stage in the last Episode as a fourth or supplementary actor, technically called a 'parachoregema'. This part might be taken by one of the slaves; and, as there is nothing to speak but a few words of barbaric jargon, he is indeed little more than a 'mute person.' The 'teacher' was always bound to give the deuteragonist and tritagonist time enough to change their apparel in the 'green-room' of the Athenian theatre; and, if in some instances that time seems scant, it must be remembered that a fresh mask was easily slipt on, and that in such cases care would be taken to make any other change of dress slight. It is, however, certain that great dramatic talent was essential, even in a tritagonist, to sustain well such a variety of characters: and (in spite of the insulting taunts levelled against Aeschines) the term 'third-rate' in modern sense would be improperly applied to such an actor. If one of the 'choreutae' spoke as a fourth actor (a resource very rarely adopted) this was called a 'paraskenium.'

ERRATUM.

Line 83, p. 10, *for* spoon *read* pot.

(For *Dramatis Personæ*, see p. lxiii.)

THE BIRDS.

SCENE: *a wild tract, with bush and rock: a tree in the distance. Enter* PEITHETAERUS *and* EUELPIDES *with slaves.*

Euelpides.
Straight, where the tree stands out—is that the track?
[*To the jay.*
Peithetaerus.
Plague take you! mine again is croaking back.

---

1. Straight, &c. (do you bid *me take* the straight *road* where the tree is visible?) 2. Plague take you (may you burst). Mine (this *crow*).

The Prologos, or introductory scene before the approach of the Chorus, extends from v. 1 to v. 220. On the scenery, characters, dresses, and divisions of the play, see Introduction.

The two Athenians, Peithetaerus and Euelpides, followed by two slaves (see v. 684), who carry their baggage, come on the stage from the (spectators') left-side entrance. Peithetaerus has a crow in his left hand, Euelpides a daw or jay. The latter, encouraged, as he fancies, by his jay, advances among the rocks. Peithetaerus, whose crow makes contrary signs, recalls him by an imprecation.

Euelpides.
Still up and down, old sinner, must we pace?
'Twill kill us both, this vain way-weaving race.

Peithetaerus.
That I, poor wretch, believing in a crow,   5
More than a thousand furlongs round should go!

Euelpides.
That I, bad luck! believing in a jay,
Should knock my wretched toe-nails all away!

Peithetaerus.
'Tis past my knowledge where on earth we stand.

Euelpides.
Could you from hence find out the fatherland?   10

Peithetaerus.
That not e'en Exekestides could do.

---

3. Old sinner (O bad *one*). 4. 'Twill, &c. (we shall perish, vainly weaving our way). 7. Bad luck (the ill-fated). 11. That not, &c. (from hence, by Jove, not even Ex. could).

---

3. "Old sinner." Terms of jocular abuse express in Attic fashion the lively familiarity of friends.

4. The metaphor in the verb (*weaving*) likens the erratic movements of the two Athenians to those of a weaver who passes the weft from one side of the loom to the other with constant alternation.

11. Exekestides (see v. 764), Akestor (v. 33), and others are ridiculed as persons who exercise or claim citizenship at Athens without legal right. It was easy to cast this slur on account of the strictness of the rules affecting legitimation. Any foreign taint on the mother's side, for instance, would expose a man to be called, in comic language, a 'barbarian,' that is, not a genuine Greek. Though the land is barbarous, and Exekestides a barbarian, even he, it is

Euelpides.

Woe, woe!

Peithetaerus.

That road, my friend, I leave to you.

Euelpides.

A scurvy trick he's played us, he o' the Birdmart,
Philokrates the poulterer, in his craze:
He said this pair would find out for us Tereus   15
The hoopoe, him that once upon a time

---

12. That road, &c. (do you indeed, my friend, go that road).

---

meant, clever inventor as he is, would not find out his native country from this spot.

12. "That road:" namely, the road of 'woe.' Ancient superstition made it usual to retort an ill-omened saying on the person who uttered it ('on your head be it').

13. "He o' the Birdmart:" lit. *he of the birds*. 'The birds' express the part of the Athenian Agora where birds were sold: so 'the fishes' for 'the fish-mart:' 'the pot-herbs' for 'the herb-mart,' 'the ointment' for 'the perfumers' booths,' &c.

14. "Poulterer:" lit. *board-salesman*. Live birds were exposed for sale having their feet fastened to a board or wooden dish.

15. Crows, daws and pyes were vulgarly supposed to have prophetic skill.

"Tereus." In the ancient myth Tereus was a Thracian king, who married Prokne, elder daughter of Pandion, king of Athens. He afterwards by fraud and force got possession of her younger sister Philomela. The sisters, plotting vengeance, murdered Itys, son of Tereus and Prokne, gave his flesh to be eaten by his father, and fled. Tereus pursued: but the gods in pity changed all three into birds. The usual legend calls Tereus a hawk, Prokne a swallow, and Philomela a nightingale: but that adopted by Aristophanes in this play makes Tereus a hoopoe, and Prokne the nightingale. Philomela is not mentioned. See Note on v. 107 (100).

Into a bird was turn'd from out the birds:
And so he sold this brat of Tharraleides,
This jay, for twopence, and yon crow for sixpence;
But all the creatures knew was—how to peck.   20
Now what do you gape at? somewhere down the rocks
Do you propose to push us? here's no road. [*To the jay.*
     Peithetaerus.
Nor here, I vow; no vestige of a path.
     Euelpides.
Your crow says something, doesn't she, of the way?

---

22 21). Do you propose to push us? (will you farther lead us?)

---

17 (16). "From out the birds." Cobet and Meincke reject this line as spurious: but this is improbable. Koechly proposes an emendation, far too bold, giving the sense 'from human form.' It may be well explained as it stands. The Greek words are the same as those rendered in v. 13, 'of the bird-mart,' and are here jocularly repeated in a different sense. We should naturally expect the phrase 'from human form:' but Aristophanes supplies one of those strokes of humour so familiar to him which are called 'counter to expectation:' and says, "from out the birds." The Greeks found in barbarian language a resemblance to the twittering of birds: Herod. II. 57, Soph. *Ant.* 1001. The analogy of bird and barbarian is often introduced by Aristophanes in this play and in others. See *Av.* 199, *Ran.* 582. Hence he may be supposed to say here, that Tereus was changed into a (winged) bird from being a (barbarian) bird.

18 (17). "Tharraleides." Most modern editors have received this form instead of the MS. reading, Tharreleides, on account of its probable derivation from the Greek 'tharraleos,' *bold, impudent.* That any person of the name existed is unlikely. The jay may be jestingly called 'a child of impudence.' Scholiasts speak of it as a nickname of one Asopodorus.

19 (18). "Twopence:" lit. *an obol*: "sixpence:" lit. *three obols*. Round sums are given in the translation; but an obol (the sixth part of an Attic drachma) was in value about three halfpence.

Peithetaerus.
Her croak is different from before, by Jove.   25
Euelpides.
But, pray, what says she of the road?
Peithetaerus.
                                                'I'll maul
And gnaw your fingers off,' she says: that's all.
Euelpides.
Now isn't it monstrous hard that, when we want
To go to the ravens, and are quite prepared,
Yet after all we can't find out the way?   30
Know, gentles, ye that come to hear our plot,
We're stricken with a certain malady,
The opposite of that which Sakas has:
He, no true citizen, is struggling in;
While we, full-franchised both in tribe and clan,   35

26—7. I'll maul, &c. (what else says she but that she will maul and eat away my fingers?)

---

29 (28). "To go to the ravens." Equivalent to our phrase 'to go to the dogs.' Ravens were supposed to prey on carcases; and all who have read Homer and Sophokles know that exposure without funeral rites was, among Greeks, a dishonour and a vengeance inflicted on the dead. 'Go to the ravens' was a common imprecation like our 'go to the deuce.'

33 (31). "Sakas." Herodotus says (VII. 64) that the Persians called all the Skythians Sakai. The name Sakas (barbarian) here designates the tragic poet Akestor, as Photius informs us. He was ridiculed also by Eupolis, Kratinus, and other comic poets.

35 (33). The division of Athenian citizens into tribes (phulai) was very ancient: but the four old Ionic tribes were enlarged to the number of ten by the constitution of Kleisthenes B.C. 510. They

Citizens in the midst of citizens,
With none to scare us, from our fatherland
Flew out, as fast as both our feet could waft us;
Not moved by hatred of that city's self,
That 'tis not in its nature great and happy, 40
And free to all alike—to pay their fines in:
No, faith! cicalas for a month or two
Are chirping on the shoots: Athenians ever
Are chirping on the suits their lifetime through.
Such are the reasons why we gang this gait: 45
With sacred corbel, pot and myrtle-sprays,
We wander, seeking for a suitless spot,

---

38 (35). As fast as, &c. (with both our feet).

---

were subdivided into boroughs or cantons (demoi). Another division was non-political, into wards (phratriai), and of these into clans or families (genea). A genuine citizen belonged to all these divisions: but the test and proof of legitimacy was the being enrolled in the register of the ward (phratria). See Grote's *History of Greece*, Part II. ch. x. and ch. xxxi.

37 (34). "Scare." The verb so rendered (sobein) is specially applied to the frightening away of birds: 'shoo, shoo.'

41, &c. (38, &c.) The litigant habits of the Athenians are ridiculed by Aristophanes, in his comedy called *The Wasps*, B.C. 422; where the chorus consists of jurymen wearing masks and stings to represent those vexatious insects.

42 (39). The chirping of cicalas on the hedges and trees of southern countries is very loud and shrill in hot weather. See Hom. *Il.* III. 152; Plat. *Phaedr.* 230, C.; Theocr. XVI. 94. So Verg. *Ecl.* II. 12, Raucis...sole sub ardenti resonant arbusta cicadis.

46 (43). These objects were ceremonially used in founding a colony. The sacred basket contained salted meal and a knife. The pot carried the holy fire from the Prytaneum of the mother-city: the myrtle-wreaths were worn by the founder during the ceremony of foundation: and also when he addressed the people.

Where we may settle down and spend our lives.
In short we're bound to Tereus' court, the hoopoe;
From him we wish to learn, if such a city   50
He e'er descried in any of his flights.

Peithetaerus.
Holloa, Sir!

Euelpides.
　　Well, what now?

Peithetaerus.
　　　　　　The crow some time
Makes upward signs to me.

Euelpides.
　　　　　　Ay, and this jay
Stares upward open-mouth'd as shewing me something.
There must be birds, no question, hereabouts: 55
But, if we make a noise, we soon shall know.

Peithetaerus.
I'll tell you what to do: just give the rock
A shin-stroke.

Euelpides.
　　By all means; and you a head-stroke;
A double knock will make a double noise.

57—9 (54—5). I'll tell you, &c. (do, do you know what? smite the rock with your leg.—Ay, and you with your head, that the noise may be double).

---

57 (54). "The rock." In the back centre of the stage appears amidst the bushes a rock, within which is the hoopoe's abode. This corresponds to the central palace gateway, shewn in most Greek plays. Two other avenues must be conceived, one on each side of the centre; of which the left leads to the nightingale's dwelling.

Peithetaerus.
Well, take a stone and strike.

Euelpides.
                       I'll do your bidding. 60
Boy, boy!

Peithetaerus.
        What's that? you call the Hoopoe 'boy'?
Ought you not rather to cry 'Hoopopoy'?

Euelpides.
Hoopopoy! whooping once, it seems, wo'nt do.
Hoopopoy!

Enter RUNNER-BIRD *from the bush.*

Runner-bird.
    Who are these? Who calls my lord?

Euelpides.
Apollo guard us! what a monstrous yawn!   65

---

65 (61). Apollo guard us (O Apollo the Averter *of evil*).

---

61 (57). "Boy, boy." The Greek 'pais,' like 'Knabe' in German, was used for *boy* or *slave*.
62 (58). "Hoopopoy." Gr. 'epopoi.' A play on the words 'epops' (hoopoe) and 'epopoiïa,' *epic poetry*.
63 (59). The word which follows 'epopoi' implies a pun, which it is intended to represent here by the word 'whoop.' Lit. *you will make me knock again*.
64 (60). The bird, which appears here as the hoopoe's page or footman, is called in Greek 'trochilos' (from 'trech-' *to run*. Some take it to mean *a wren;* others *a wagtail*. His mask exhibits a beak with a very wide expanse; see v. 65. Perhaps he has wings, but the rest of his dress is probably that of a slave at Athens.

Runner-bird.
Me miserable! they're a brace of fowlers.
Euelpides.
So foul a thing is scarce polite to utter.
Runner-bird.
You'll both be put to death.
Euelpides.
    But we're not men.
Runner-bird.
What are you?
Euelpides.
  Funkling I, a Libyan bird.
Runner-bird.
All fudge!
Euelpides.
  You'll find abundant evidence.   70
Runner-bird.
Well, and what bird's this other? wo'nt you speak?
Peithetaerus.
Skunkling am I, one of the Telltale tits.
Euelpides.
But pr'ythee say, what animal are you?
Runner-bird.
I am a slave-bird.
Euelpides.
  Did' some cock defeat you?

---

72 (68). "One of the Telltale tits." Lit. *a Phasian* bird. The word *Phasian* suggests the double notion of *pheasant* and *informer*.

74 (70). Cock-fighting and quail-fighting were fashionable at Athens. Prisoners of war were often sold into slavery.

Runner-bird.
Not so: but when my lord became a hoopoe,   75
He prayed that I too might become a bird;
So should he have a pursuivant and page.
Euelpides.
One bird then needs another for a page?
Runner-bird.
My master does, by reason, I suppose,
That he was formerly a man; and so,   80
When he would lunch upon Phalerian whitebait,
I run to fetch him whitebait, dish in hand.
Soup if he craves, ladle and spoon are wanted:
I run for a ladle.
Euelpides.
'Tis the Runner-bird.
I'll tell you, Runner, what to do: go call   85
Your master for us.
Runner-bird.
Nay, but he's just gone
To take a nap after a hearty meal
Of myrtle-berries, with a gnat or two.
Euelpides.
Well, wake him all the same.
Runner-bird.
I'm very sure
He'll be displeas'd, but for your sakes I'll wake him.   90
[*Exit Runner-bird.*

---

81 (76). 'Aphuai,' small sprats or anchovies, here called *whitebait*, were caught off the Phalerian or Eastern port of Athens.

Peithetaerus.
Go and be hang'd, for frightening me to death.
Euelpides.
Woe's me, unlucky wight! my jay too's gone
In terror.
Peithetaerus.
O you biggest of big cowards,
Your fright it was allowed the jay to go.
Euelpides.
Pray didn't you tumble down and loose the crow? 95
Peithetaerus.
Not I, by Jove.
Euelpides.
Where is she?
Peithetaerus.
Flown away.
Euelpides.
Oh, you didn't loose her, bravest of the brave.

The Hoopoe speaks from the bush.
Hoopoe.
Open the greenwood, that I may come forth.

Enter HOOPOE.
Euelpides.
Great Herakles! what animal is here?
What plumage this? what triple-crested fashion? 100

---

91 (85). Go and be hang'd (may you perish miserably). 97 (91). Bravest of the brave (you are so valiant, good *Sir*).

---

100 (94). The hoopoe's costume seems to have been both grotesque and brilliant. He wears a mask, with a ludicrous beak

Hoopoe.

Who are they that come to seek me?

Euelpides.

The twelve gods—
Seem to have smash'd you.

Hoopoe.

Strangers, do you flout me,
Because you see this plumage? I was once
A man.

Euelpides.

We do not laugh at you.

Hoopoe.

What then?

Euelpides.

That beak of yours looks to us laughable. 105

Hoopoe.

Of course: such insult in his tragedies
Does Sophokles inflict on me, the Tereus.

(v. 105) and upon it, apparently, a bunch of feathers, surmounted with a high triple crest. In other respects he has a human form and a dress of glaring colours (vv. 108—9).

101—2 (95—6). Here is a joke of the class mentioned on v. 17. Euelp. pretends to answer the question of the hoopoe by the words, *the twelve gods,*—but roguishly adds, *seem to have smashed you.* 'May you be smashed'! is one of the many Greek forms of imprecation. See v. 1530. 'The greater gods' were twelve in number.

107 (100). The tragedy of Sophokles called Tereus was probably well known, though of uncertain date; its highly tragic plot would be worked out by the great dramatist with the consummate skill which we find in his extant plays. We may surmise that in the last scene one of the deities, probably Hermes, arrests the infuriated prince, and announces to him his coming metamor-

Euelpides.
You're Tereus, are you? bird or peacock, which?

Hoopoe.
A bird am I.

Euelpides.
Where are your feathers, then?

Hoopoe.
They've fallen off.

Euelpides.
Was that from some disease?   110

Hoopoe.
No: in the winter all birds moult their feathers,
And then again we fledge another set.
But tell me what you twain are.

Euelpides.
Mortals we.

---

phosis, with the changes of Prokne and Philomela. The particulars of his new form, 'the terrors of his beak and lightnings of his eye,' may have been there described : and of such a description the hoopoe may here complain as insulting. It suits the purpose of Aristophanes to exhibit Tereus in a different aspect, as a powerful and friendly bird-prince, and husband of the gentle and melodious nightingale, once the Athenian princess Prokne. Hence the Sophoklean legend, fresh in the memory of the audience, is set aside by the hoopoe as defaming his character.

108 (102) "Bird or peacock." The ordinary word for bird (ornis) sometimes means the domestic fowl or hen. The peacock was a novelty rarely brought to Athens from the East at this time, (*Acharn.* 61), and, as a kind of monster, is here ridiculously distinguished from 'bird.' So again v. 287 (269).

Hoopoe.
Your native country?
Euelpides.
Whence the gallant triremes.
Hoopoe.
Heliasts, are you?
Euelpides.
No, the other sort,   115
Heliast-haters.
Hoopoe.
Is that seed sown there?
Euelpides.
A sprinkling you may gather off the field.
Hoopoe.
But, pray, what object come you here in quest of?
Euelpides.
An interview with you.
Hoopoe.
Upon what business?
Euelpides.
Seeing that, first, you once were man, like us,   120
Once money owed to creditors, like us,

115—16 (109—10). The supreme Athenian judicature was called Heliaea, and the jurymen (dikasts) who served in it Heliasts. See Grote's *Hist.* II. Ch. xxxi. Aristophanes here coins a word 'Apeliasts,' to express shunners or haters of the Heliaea, that is, of litigation.

117 (111). Some commentators find here an allusion to the simpler and more virtuous character of the rural population. This seems doubtful.

Once gladly shirk'd repaying it, like us;
Next, changing to the nature of the birds,
You flew about o'er land and sea, and all
The feelings both of man and bird are yours,   125
Therefore we're hither come as suppliants to you,
To see if you can shew us some snug city,
Soft as a blanket to lie down and snooze in.

Hoopoe.

A greater city seek you than the Kranaan?

Euelpides.

Not greater, no; but nicer for ourselves.   130

Hoopoe.

You seek an aristocracy, that's clear.

Euelpides.

Not I: and Skellias' youngster makes me sick.

Hoopoe.

What kind of city would you choose to dwell in?

Euelpides.

One where the greatest troubles should be these:

---

129 (123). "The Kranaan." This old name for Athens (the rocky) was pleasing to the popular ear. Kranaus ranks among the mythic heroes of Athens, as stepson and successor of its founder Kekrops.

132 (126). Aristokrates, son of Skellias, played a not unimportant part in Athenian politics after the date of this play. He was one of the oligarchy of four hundred established at Athens by the conspiracy of B.C. 411. But he concurred with Theramenes in resisting the treasonable designs of the more violent oligarchs, and in demolishing the fort of Eetioneia. See Thuk. VIII. 89. He was among the six unfortunate commanders executed at Athens B.C. 406 for having neglected to succour the wrecked Athenian ships at the close of the battle of Arginusae.

Some friend should seek my door at morning tide,   135
And say, 'By Zeus Olympius I beseech,
You and your children take an early bath,
And visit me: I give a wedding breakfast;
Don't think of saying no, or, if you do,
Never approach me, when my fortunes ebb.'   140

Hoopoe.
Good sooth, sad troubles you're enamoured of.
And you?
Peithetaerus.
My longing is the same.

Hoopoe.
For what?

Peithetaerus.
One where a friend should meet me in the street,
The father of a marriageable daughter,   144
And rate me soundly thus, as having wronged him:
'Stilbonides, you never come to see
My little girl; I'll whisper in your ear,
She'll have five talents for her marriage-portion;
And you're my old hereditary friend.'

---

137 (132). Bathing before meals, especially before a banquet, was the usual practice at Athens. See *Lysist.* 1064.

140 (134). "Ebb." A jocular inversion of the ordinary proverb. The following line is ironical; as again, v. 150.

146 (139) "Stilbonides." This is an imaginary name adopted here by Peithetaerus: but there is nothing to account for the selection of it.

146—8. Part of this speech is substituted, not translated.

Hoopoe.

Poor fellow, what afflictions you're in love with! 150
Well, there's a city such as you describe,
Favoured of fortune, on the Red-sea coast.

Euelpides.

Ah! name it not: no seaside place for us,
Where sudden, some fine morning, will pop up,
Carrying a summoner, the Salaminia. 155
But can you tell us some Hellenic city?

Hoopoe.

Why don't you go to Lepreus of Elis,
And there reside?

---

152 (145). "On the Red-sea coast." The Happy Land of the ancients was sometimes imagined in the extreme East, as here, where Red-sea means the Persian gulph, sometimes among the Hyperboreans (see Pind. *Pyth.* x.); sometimes in the farthest West, the Fortunate Islands. So the Middle Ages had their fanciful Eldorado, realized in some measure by the discovery of America and Australia.

155 (147). "The Salaminia." Athens had two state triremes, Paralus and Salaminia. The latter was used to send officers for the arrest of accused persons. Aristophanes alludes to the recall and attempted arrest of Alkibiades by the home government on the charge of sacrilege and treason in the affair of the Hermokopidae. This had occurred shortly before the production of *The Birds*. See Thuk. VI. 6. Grote's *Hist. of Greece*, II. Ch. lviii.

157 (149). Lepreum or Lepreus was a town of Triphylian Elis. See Grote's *Hist.*, II. Ch. lv. It suggests the idea of Melanthius, who was afflicted with a *leprous* eruption. This Melanthius was a tragic poet, son of Philokles, and had already, with his brother Morsimus, fallen under the lash of Aristophanes in *The Peace* (v. 804, 1009) as a coarse epicure. He was ridiculed also by the comic writers Pherekrates, Eupolis, Archippus, and others.

Euelpides.
Because, so witness heaven,
Although I never saw it, from Melanthius
The very name of Lepreus turns my stomach. 160
Hoopoe.
In Lokris there's another breed, Opuntians,
Where you should settle.
Euelpides.
To become Opuntius,
No, not a talent's weight of gold would tempt me.
But what's the style of living with the birds?
You know it well, no doubt.
Hoopoe.
Not disagreeable 165
For daily wear and tear: to take an instance,
You have to live without a purse.
Euelpides.
Good riddance
Of one of life's most palpable corruptions!
Hoopoe.
We feed in gardens on white sesame-grains,
On myrtle-berries, poppy-seed, and water-mint. 170
Euelpides.
Then 'tis a life of bridegrooms that you lead.

---

167 (158). Good, &c. (you remove a great adulteration of life).

161 (152). The Lokri Opuntii, so called from Opus, their capital, suggest the name of Opuntius, an ugly one-eyed person.
171 (161). "Bridegrooms." Of the vegetables here named some were used in the decoration of wedding-feasts, others in the food, as sesame and poppy-seeds.

Peithetaerus.

Huzza! huzza!
I spy a great design, I really do,
Within the scope of birds to frame, and power
To work it out, if you will only take   175
My counsel.

Hoopoe.

Take what counsel?

Peithetaerus.

What? why first
Cease flying all about with open bills:
Such conduct's not respectable. For instance,
In our world there inquire about the flutterers,
'Who's yonder fellow?' Teleas will reply,   180
'Oh, that's a bird-man flying without ballast,
All aimless, never staying in one spot.'

Hoopoe.

Right well you ridicule such ways, by Bacchus.
What must we do, then?

Peithetaerus.

Found a single city.

Hoopoe.

What sort of city could we found, we birds?   185

---

180 (168). "Teleas." Nothing is really known of this person. He is mentioned again, v. 1025, as giving a public commission. Hence it may be conjectured that he held some position in the Athenian police.

Peithetaerus.
So, so? you speaker of the silliest speech,
Look down.
          Hoopoe.
    I'm looking.
               Peithetaerus.
          Now look up.
          Hoopoe.
                   I do.
        Peithetaerus.
Now turn your neck about.
           Hoopoe.
              A pretty gain
'Twill be, forsooth, if I'm to wring my neck.
          Peithetaerus.
Did you see something?
           Hoopoe.
          Yes; the clouds and sky.   190
        Peithetaerus.
These constitute, I think, the site of birds.
          Hoopoe.
'Site!' how do you mean?
          Peithetaerus.
          Another term for 'seat.'

    191—196 (179—184). The *jeu de mots* in these lines is preserved by substituting for three Greek words (polos, topos, poleitai) three English words 'site,' 'seat,' 'sight,' with which the word 'city' (polis) happens to correspond sufficiently.

There's such a sight of things within their range,
That now they're naturally called 'a site;'
But, settled once, and fortified by you,   195
Instead of 'site' they shall be term'd 'a city.'
So will ye rule o'er men as over locusts,
And wear the gods to death with Melian famine.

Hoopoe.

How so?

Peithetaerus.

The air's midway, methinks, from earth:
And just as, if we want to visit Delphi,   200
We ask Boeotians for a passage through,
Even so, whene'er men sacrifice to gods,
Unless the gods agree to pay you tribute,
You'll not let savoury meat-steams pass your way.

Hoopoe.

Bravo! bravo!   205
By earth, by snares, by gins, by nets, I never—
No, never did I hear a prettier notion:

---

198 (186). "Melian famine." The Athenians had blockaded the isle of Melos, and starved it into surrender two years before, B.C. 416.

200 (189). At Delphi, in Phokis, was the great temple of the Pythian Apollo; and the road to it from Athens lay through Boeotia. Hence the Athenians, when they wished to attend the games or consult the oracle, were obliged to seek permission from their enemies the Thebans to pass through Boeotian territory.

206 (194). As swearing is the attestation of a superior and dreaded power, Aristophanes jestingly makes the hoopoe swear by nets and snares of which he stands in awe.

So with your help the city will I found,
Consent being given by the other birds.

Peithetaerus.
Who will expound the matter to them?

Hoopoe.
You shall: 210
For, though they were a barbarous race before,
I taught them language, living with them long.

Peithetaerus.
How then can you convoke them?

Hoopoe.
Easily.
I'll enter here at once into the bush,
And after I've aroused my nightingale, 215
We'll call them. If they do but hear our voice,
They'll run full speed.

Peithetaerus.
Then stay not, dearest bird,
But, I beseech you, go into the bush
This instant, and arouse the nightingale.

[*The Hoopoe enters the bush and chants.*

Hoopoe.
Cease, my mate, from slumber now; 220

---

220 (209). The hoopoe goes into the bush by the left back entrance towards the nightingale's abode and chants the invocation to her. Afterwards he returns and approaches the right back entrance from which he chants the lines summoning the birds, v. 241, &c. These two songs (asmata) wind up the Prologos and lead to the Parodos.

Let the sacred hymn-notes flow,
Wailing with thy voice divine
Long-wept Itys, mine and thine.
So, when thy brown beak is thrilling
With that holy music-trilling,   225
Through the woodbine's leafy bound
Swells the pure melodious sound
To the throne of Zeus: and there
Phoebus of the golden hair,
Hearing, to thine elegies   230
With the awaken'd chords replies
Of his ivory-claspèd lyre,
Stirring all the Olympian quire;
Till from each immortal tongue
Of that blessèd heavenly throng   235
Peals the full harmonious song.

[*Music is played, imitating the notes of the
nightingale.*]

Euelpides.
O royal Zeus! that bird's voice! what a flood
Of honey did it stream o'er all the wood!

Peithetaerus.
Holloa, Sir!

Euelpides.
Well, what now?

Peithetaerus.
Be silent.

Euelpides.
Why?

Peithetaerus.

The Hoopoe frames another melody.   240

Hoopoe.

Epopopopopopopopopopopopopoi!
Holloa! holloa! what ho! what ho!
Hither haste, my plume-partakers;
Come many, come any
That pasture on the farmer's well-sown acres,   245
Tribes countless that on barley feed,
And clans that gather out the seed;
Come, alert upon the wing,
Dulcet music uttering:
Ye that o'er the furrowed sod   250
Twitter upon every clod,
Making all the air rejoice
With your soft and slender voice:
Tio, tio, tio, tio, tio, tio, tio, tio.
Ye that feast on garden fruits,   255
Nestling 'midst the ivy shoots:
Ye that all the mountains throng,
Olive-croppers, arbute-loppers,
Haste and fly to greet my song.
Trioto, trioto, totobrix!   260
Ye that o'er the marshy flats
Swallow down the shrill-mouthed gnats;
Ye that haunt the deep-dew'd ground
Marathon's sweet meads around,

Ouzel, and thou of the speckled wing, 265
Hazelhen, hazelhen, speed while I sing.
Come many, come any
With the halcyon brood that sweep
Surges of the watery deep,
Come and list to novel words, 270
Which to hear, from far and near
We gather all the tribes of neckextending birds.
Here is arrived a sharp old man
Of revolutionary mind,
To revolutionary deeds inclined: 275
Come all, and listen to his plan.
Hither, hither, hither, hither,
Torotorotorotorotix,
Kikkabau kikkabau,
Torotorotorotorolililix. 280

Peithetaerus.

See you some bird?

Euelpides.

By Apollo, no, not I:
Yet all agape I'm gazing on the sky.

---

265 (249). The correction of Meineke, followed by Holden, is here adopted. It introduces a bird called 'pterōn,' rendered *ouzel* (as 'attagas' *hazelhen*), but the names are dubious.

272 (254). "Neckextending." Characteristic epithet.

281 (263). Here we have the preparation for the Parodos or arrival of the Chorus, which actually commences at v. 312. The two Athenians look about them for birds: at last one appears (v. 285), about which they question the hoopoe, who has returned to the logeion.

Peithetaerus.

So then the Hoopoe went into the wood
And mocked the curlew's screaming for no good.

Bird entering.

Torotix, torotix. 285

Peithetaerus.

Nay, my friend; this very moment here's a bird approaching close.

---

284 (266). "Curlew." The bird here mentioned (charadrius) is afterwards (1141) called a river-bird. Aristotle says it builds in rocks and near cataracts. But naturalists have not certainly identified it.

285—322 (267—304). The four birds which first appear do not belong to the Chorus, but come through the stage entrance (or entrances) on the right (of the spectators) and retire again. The first is a flamingo (v. 291). The second, which the hoopoe calls Medus (that is, the Persian bird), is some variety of our domestic cock, brought to Greece from the East. The third is an imaginary variety of the hoopoe, invented to suit a comic purpose. The fourth, here called Gobbler, is likewise a mere invention, ridiculing Kleonymus. All four were no doubt brilliantly and fantastically got up. The twenty-four birds afterwards mentioned, beginning with the partridge and ending with the woodchat, constitute the Chorus. They enter the orchestra by the right-hand parodos and array themselves on the platform. Either they represent birds by their masks only, or they may also shew rudimental wings; but body and feet are human, with dresses various, rich and ludicrous. The special mention of the owl at v. 319, and its dignity as the bird of Pallas Athene, lead to the conjecture that it plays the part of coryphaeus or speaker of the Chorus. Of the birds enumerated some can be certainly recognized by English names: as the partridge, owl, pye, turtle, lark, pigeon, hawk, cuckoo, falcon, diver, osprey. For the rest, which are unknown, English substitutes are adopted.

Euelpides.

Ay, by Jove! what bird, I wonder? 'Tis a peacock, I suppose.

Peithetaerus.

Our obliging friend will tell us. What's this bird, Sir? kindly say.

Hoopoe.

'Tis not one of those accustomed sorts you're seeing every day,
But a lake-bird.

Euelpides.

O the beauty! What a brilliant tint of flame!   290

Hoopoe.

And a very proper colour, for 'flamingo' is its name.

Euelpides.

Holloa, you Sir!

Peithetaerus.

What d'ye bawl at?

Euelpides.

Here's another coming now.

Peithetaerus.

Yes, another bird, and 'holding an uncommon site,' I vow.

---

287. "Peacock." See note on v. 108.

291 (273). "Flamingo:" Gr. 'phoenikopteros,' i.e. scarlet-wing. Hence in v. 290, lit. 'how beautiful and scarlet-coloured!'

293 (275). "Holding an uncommon site." Words taken from the second *Tyro* of Sophokles: they here mean 'out of the common way.'

Pray, Sir, what is that absurd delicate-treading muse-
seer bird?

Hoopoe.

Medus is its native title.

Euelpides.

Medus?   Herakles the king!
Flying in without a camel! Could a Mede do such a
thing?   296

Peithetaerus.

Here's another bird that's taken to himself a crest
again.

---

296 (278). Flying in, &c. (how then, being a Mede, did he fly in without a camel?)   297 (279). Taken to himself (seized).

---

294 (276). Some editors divide this verse between Peithetaerus and Hoopoe. 'Who is this, Sir?—'Tis the absurd, &c.' This seems improbable. The epithets suggested to Peithetaerus by the appearance of the cock are unsuited to the hoopoe's reply. The term "absurd" is already contained in the tragic citation v. 293. "Delicate-treading" is drawn from the strutting air of the cock, which brings to mind the oriental gait. Why the cock is called "muse-seer" by Peithetaerus is not so obvious: perhaps his pompous manner of crowing suggests the solemn delivery of an oracle.

296 (278). The Persian wars had introduced the camel to the knowledge of the Greeks. Hence a Mede is jocularly supposed by Aristophanes to require a camel, even when flying on the stage as a bird.

297 (279). Here is a play on the Greek noun (lophos), which, like the English 'crest,' may refer to a helmet or to a hill. Hence the choice of the word "taken," which slightly keeps up the double sense. It seems to prepare for the continuation of the joke in v. 311.

Euelpides.

Hey! what's this by way of marvel? Are not you
   sole Hoopoe, then?
Have you got a double, please?

Hoopoe.

                        This is son of Philokles,
Son of Hoopoe: I'm his grandsire: like your own our
   titles run,   300
Kallias son of Hipponikus, Hipponikus Kallias' son.

Euelpides.

Kallias then this bird you call: see how fast his feathers
   fall.

Hoopoe.

Yes, because he is a lordling, parasites his plumage
   clip;
And the lady-birds moreover all the little remnant strip.

---

   299 (281). Have you got a double, please? (but is this too a second?)
300 (282). Like your own, &c. (as if you were to say).

---

   299 (281). "Son of Philokles." The explanation of this difficult place, according to the Scholiast, is as follows. Philokles was a prolific tragic poet, sister's son to Aeschylus. He wrote a tetralogy called *Pandionis*, in which was contained the story of Tereus. The hoopoe, as appears from v. 107, identifies himself with the Tereus of Sophokles, though dissatisfied with his own portraiture in the drama of that poet. He seems to say, 'I am the original Hoopoe (of Sophokles), and Philokles a son of mine (which may mean that Philokles plagiarized from Sophokles) who has produced another Hoopoe, so called from his grandsire, by a fashion familiar to the great houses at Athens.' This leads to identification of the featherless hoopoe minor with Kallias son of Hipponikus, a dissolute young man, whose sister married Alkibiades. For other opinions on the passage, see Appendix.

Euelpides.

O Poseidon! here's another particoloured bird in sight:
What's the title we're to give him?

Hoopoe.
Call him Gobbler, and you're right. 306

Euelpides.
Gobbler is there any known save Kleonymus alone?

Peithetaerus.
If Kleonymus we call him, ought he not his crest to lose?

Euelpides.
Well, but whence arose this fashion of the birds, a crest to use?
Went they to the double-heat race?

Hoopoe.
No, good Sir, they build their nests 310
With a view to preservation, like the Karians, upon crests.

---

307 (289). Kleonymus is ridiculed as a tall handsome man, but gluttonous, mean and cowardly, who fled from battle without his shield.

310 (292). In the double-heat race (diaulos dromos) the racers ran round the goal back to the starting-place. Sometimes it was an armed race, in which the panoply of the hoplite was worn. To such a race is the allusion here.

311 (292). Herodotus (I. 171) says that the Karians invented the fashion of wearing crests on helmets. Aristophanes jocularly calls it dwelling on crests, because the Karians, like the old Italian tribes, built their towns on hill-tops.

Peithetaerus.
O Poseidon! what a plaguy lot of birds are gather'd here!
Don't you see?
Euelpides.
O king Apollo, what a cloud! O dear! O dear!
For their flying now no more can we see the entrance-door.
Hoopoe.
Hither is a partridge coming, there a hazelhen is shewn;
Upon this side is a widgeon: upon that a halcyon. 316
Peithetaerus.
What's the one we see behind her?
Hoopoe.
That one? Razorbill's the name.
Peithetaerus.
Razorbill's a bird then?
Euelpides.
Call it Sporgilus, 'twill be the same.
Hoopoe.
Here's an owl.
Peithetaerus.
What's this you tell me? Who to Athens brought an owl?

---

314 (296). "The entrance-door." The right-hand parodos of the orchestra is here implied.

317 (299). A certain seabird, properly 'kerulos,' is here called 'keirulos' (cutting-bird or razorbill), which suggests the mention of an Athenian barber Sporgilus.

319 (301). To bring an owl to Athens (where so many coins

Hoopoe.

Pye and turtle, lark and pigeon, goatsucker and guinea-
 fowl, 320
Hawk and falcon, cushat, cuckoo, redshank, redpole,
 come in view,
Gannet, kestrel, diver, osprey, flycatcher, and woodchat too.

Euelpides.

Merrily, merrily come the birds, merrily come the blackbirds all:
What a twittering! what a fluttering! what variety of
 squall!
Don't they threaten us? I fear so: sure with yawning
 beaks they blink, 325
And on you and me are staring.

Peithetaerus.

You are right, I really think.

Chorus.

Wh--- wh--- wh--- wh--- where is he summon'd me?
 in what region feedeth he?

Hoopoe.

Here am I long time expecting: from my friends I
 never flee.

323—4 (305—7). (Oho, oho the birds! oho, oho the blackbirds! how they chirp and run crying variously!)

---

and sculptures bore the image of the bird of Pallas Athene) was a proverb conveying the same idea as 'carrying coals to Newcastle' in English. The joke is heightened by making Peithetaerus forget that he is not now at Athens, but in Birdland.

Chorus.

T--- t--- t--- t--- tell me, pray, what to-day friendly
word have you to say?

Hoopoe.

One that's safe and just and pleasant and of public
use, you'll find: 330
Here are two men come to see me, schemers both, of
subtle mind.

Chorus.

Where? which way? what do you say?

Hoopoe.

Two old men are come, I answer, hither from the Isle
of Man:
And they bring a business with them, solid, of enormous span.

Chorus.

O you worst of all offenders since I first began to feed,
What do you tell me?

Hoopoe.

Don't be frighten'd.

Chorus.

What is this unfriendly deed?   336

Hoopoe.

I've receiv'd two men, enamoured of a social league
with you.

---

333 (330). From the Isle of Man (from men).

Chorus.
So you've really gone and done it?
Hoopoe.
Ay, and very gladly too.
Chorus.
And are they now somewhere near us?
Hoopoe.
Yes, if I am near to you.
Chorus.
Alas, alas! betrayed are we,   340
Treated with impiety:
He who was our friend, who feeds
Near us in our common meads,
All our ancient rules forsaking,
All the oaths of birds is breaking;   345
Lures me to a treacherous place,
Sells me to an impious race,
Which was ever unto me
Bred in mortal enmity,
Since it first began to be.   350
But we shall proceed to reckon with the bird another day;
For these two old men, I'd have them now the penal forfeit pay,
And be torn in pieces by us.

Peithetaerus.
There! all's up with us, you see.
Euelpides.
Yes, and you alone must answer for our dire calamity.
For what purpose did you lead me thence?

Peithetaerus.
That you might follow me. 355
Euelpides.
Nay, that I might cry my eyes out.
Peithetaerus.
Pack of nonsense that about
Crying; how are you to do it when your eyes are once
torn out?
Chorus.
Ho! forward! march, advance the deadly warlike charge:
Throw out both wings, and to outflank, our front enlarge:
Since the twain must weep and cry, 360
And pasture to the beak supply.
For nor shady mountain lair,
Nor the cloud that sails in air,
Nor any depth of hoary sea
May shelter them escaped from me. 365
So let us delay no longer both our foes to tear and
bite;
Where's the general of division? let him straight lead
on our right.

358 (343), &c. The Birds, displeased at the reception of men, prepare to assail the two Athenians, who, arming themselves with their cooking utensils, and supported by their slaves, stand on the defensive.

367 (353). "General of division:" taxiarch. There were ten taxiarchs at Athens commanding the infantry of the ten tribes, and ten phylarchs commanding the cavalry: all under the ten strategi or board of generals in chief (war-office). This function is jocularly transferred to the **Birds**. See Grote, Part II. Ch. viii.

Euelpides.
'Tis the crisis: whither wretched can I fly?

Peithetaerus.
What, won't you stay?

Euelpides.
To be torn in pieces by them?

Peithetaerus.
Can you then invent a way
To escape?

Euelpides.
I know none.

Peithetaerus.
Then I'll tell you how to manage it: 370
We must make a standing fight, and take some pots
from out our kit.

Euelpides.
And what good's a pot to do us?

Peithetaerus.
This the owl will not molest.

Euelpides.
But for these crooktalon'd wretches?

Peithetaerus.
Grasp the spit, and let it rest

---

371 (357). The pots (chutrai) seem to be here used first as helmets, and afterwards, with the platters, as ramparts.

372 (358). The owl will not molest the pot, because on Athenian coins the owl was perched on a pot, which was called an invention of Pallas; and the pot was carried in procession at the Panathenæa.

In your front full firmly planted.

Euelpides.
For the eyes what must be done?

Peithetaerus.
Take a saucer or a platter out, and tie it tightly on.

Euelpides.
O you cleverest of commanders, all your plan is well
 design'd; 376
In the art of engineering you've left Nikias far behind.

Chorus.
Eleleleu, quick march, present the beak; no moment
 for delay:
Haul 'em, tear 'em, smite 'em, flay 'em, striking first
 the pot away.

Hoopoe.
Vilest of the brute creation, tell me, would you slay
 and skin 380
Two men who have never harm'd you, of my lady's
 tribe and kin?

Chorus.
Spare them? spare the wolves then: can we punish a
 more hostile kind?

---

382 (369). Spare them? spare the wolves then (why should we spare these more than wolves?)

---

377 (363). Nikias was highly esteemed for his skill in conducting sieges. See Thuk. III. 51. VI.

378 (364). The Birds are about to charge, but the Hoopoe, interposing, persuades them to give audience to Peithetaerus.

Hoopoe.

Hostile if they are by nature, yet they bear a friendly mind,
And a thing they're come to teach us we may to our profit find.

Chorus.

Can it be then to our profit, any tale by these men told,
Any lesson of their teaching, foemen to my sires of old? 386

Hoopoe.

Much instruction do the wise gather from their enemies:
'Good precaution's sure salvation:' this from friends you never learn;
But your foeman puts the screw on, and 'tis taught you to a turn.
Foes, not friends, instructed nations fortresses and fleets to make: 390
And this lesson saves their children, homes, and all they have at stake.

Chorus.

Well, indeed, in my opinion, giving audience to their speech
May be useful to begin with: something wise a foe may teach.

Peithetaerus.

Now their wrath they seem to slacken; so retire a step or two.

---

389 (377). But your foeman &c. (but the enemy compels immediately.)
390 (378). (Cities for instance learnt from foes and not friends to build up high walls and to acquire ships of war.)

---

397 (386), &c. The Athenians still maintain a defensive position, while the Hoopoe explains to the chorus the mission of Pei-

Hoopoe.
What you said is common justice, and your thanks to
 me are due. 395
Chorus.
Ne'er on any other question have we been opposed
 to you.
Peithetaerus.
They're more peaceful than before; so the pot and
 dishes lower:
For the spear (I mean the spit), we must still be
 holding it,
As we pace the encampment, peeping
O'er the kettle's rim, and keeping 400
Good look out: we must not fly.

Euelpides.
In what soil, then, if we die,
Tell me, shall we buried lie?

Peithetaerus.
Burial-place for you and me
Shall the Kerameikus be: 405

---

404 (395). (The Kerameikus will receive us; for that we may be publicly buried, we will say to the strategi, &c)

---

thetaerus. They then consent to a truce, which they confirm by oath.
 398—401 (388—392). There is probably some corruption in the Greek: but the meaning must be nearly that here expressed.
 405 (395). "Kerameikus;" Potter's ground. The public funerals

Public funeral to secure,
We shall the war-office tell,
'Fighting with the foe we fell
In the battle of Birdpûr.'

Chorus.

Now again your steps retrace; 410
Wheel into your former place:
Stooping there in hoplite fashion
Ground your temper next your passion,
That by inquiry we may find
Whence come this pair, and with what mind. 415
Sir Hoopoe, you I call: what ho!

Hoopoe.

What does your calling seek to know?

Chorus.

Who are these? whence come they? tell us.

Hoopoe.

Strangers they from clever Hellas.

---

of those slain in battle were celebrated in the outer Kerameikus at Athens. See Thuk. II. 34, with the notes of commentators.

409 (399). "In the battle of Birdpûr:" lit. 'at Orneae;' a play on 'ornea,' *birds*. Orneae, a town in Argolis, was besieged by the Athenians and Argives two years before this play was acted; but as the garrison evacuated the town in the night, there was no fighting, and no lives lost; which adds zest to the joke here.

413 (401). Instead of saying 'ground your spear beside your shield,' like the 'hoplite' or heavy-armed soldier, they are jocularly made to say 'ground your temper beside your passion' or anger.

Chorus.
To the birds what fortune brings 'em? 420
Hoopoe.
Love of birds and birdlife stings 'em.
Dwellers with you they would be,
Ever of your company.
Chorus.
What's this story that you tell?
What proposals do they make? 425
Hoopoe.
Incredible, incredible,
Far too large for ears to take.
Chorus.
Sees he then a chance of gaining
Any good by here remaining?
Does he certainly confide, 430
Dwelling ever at my side,
 To o'erthrow
 Any foe,
 Any friend
 To defend? 435

420, &c. (410, &c.). (The desire of what fortune brings them to visit the birds?—Of your life and habits, and of dwelling with you and being with you entirely?)
427 (416). Far too, &c. (beyond hearing).

---

430 (417). Here and afterwards the chorus speak in the singular of Peithetaerus only, as the principal planner.

Hoopoe.
He predicts for you and me
Some immense felicity,
Not by language to be taught,
Not to be conceiv'd in thought.
He will prove by reasons strong   440
All these things to you belong,
All that's here and all that's hither,
All that's there and all that's thither.

Chorus.
What? is he a brainsick fool?

Hoopoe.
Monstrous sensible and cool.   445

Chorus.
Has he learnt a trick or two?

Hoopoe.
'Cutest fox I ever knew
Plans and precedents to show'r,
Smooth as butter, fine as flour.

Chorus.
His proposals unto me   450
   Bid him utter, utter,
Listening to the tale, you see,
   Sets me all a-flutter.

---

438 (422). Not by, &c. (neither utterable nor credible.)
444, &c. (426, &c.). (Is he mad then?—Unspeakably sensible.—Is there wisdom in his heart?—*He is* a very deep fox, a sophism, a success, an old hand, and mere fine flour.)

Hoopoe.

Now you and you this panoply take back
And hang it up, in prospect of good luck, 455
Within the kitchen by the plate-rack's side.
And you, Sir, make the statements, which to hear
I summon'd these: expound.

Peithetaerus.

Not I, by Apollo!
Unless they make the covenant with me,
Which with his wife that ape the swordwright made,
That they won't bite or worry me; in short, 461
Won't scratch my eyes out.

Chorus.

Good: I covenant.

Peithetaerus.

Then swear it.

Chorus.

Well, I swear: if I am faithful,

---

463 (445). (I swear on these conditions: *that I* conquer by all the judges and all the spectators.—This shall be so.—But, should I transgress, that I conquer by one judge only.)

---

454 (435). The hoopoe speaks to the two Athenian slaves: and as the panoply of their masters consists of pots, spits, &c., he bids them take all into his kitchen, and hang them up near the 'epistates,' a term variously explained as 'a bust of the fire-god Hephaestus,' 'a boiler,' 'a meatscreen' or 'hastener,' 'a plate-rack,' which last interpretation is here adopted, as on the whole most probable.

460 (440). "That ape." The person meant is a cutler named Panaetius, of dwarfish size, whose wife ill-used him, until he forced her to make a covenant of good behaviour.

463 (445). "If I am faithful." These words, though not expressed in the Greek, are necessarily implied.

Then, by the votes of all the judges here,
And all spectators, the first prize be mine. 465

Peithetaerus.

Accepted.

Chorus.

But, if I transgress the oath,
Then by one judge's casting-vote—I win.

Hoopoe.

Oyez, oyez! let every hoplite now
Take up his armour and go home again,
And note our proclamations on the signboards. 470

Chorus.

At every time, on every side, *Strophe.*
Man's crafty nature is descried.
Yet freely speak your mind:
For haply you may find

---

468 (448). Oyez, oyez (hear, O people).

---

467 (447). "I win." He ought to say 'I lose:' but by an unexpected joke the condition is reversed.

468 (448). "Oyez." The regular form of disbanding soldiers for the time, as used by the strategus, is here jocularly placed in the Hoopoe's mouth.

471, &c. (451, &c.). After a short Chorikon, of which the Antistrophe is at v. 566 (539), Peithetaerus, as a skilful rhetorician, undertakes to prove, by a series of ludicrous arguments, that the Birds are the true original deities, and the Olympian gods usurpers. This forms the First Episode. See Introduction.

471 (451). The Birds confess man's superior insight, and declare their wish to hear Peithetaerus.

Some useful character in me, 475
Some mightier faculty,
To which my witless thoughts ne'er travelled,
By your acuter sense unravelled.
Such vantage-ground if you have found,
Unto the public ear the case expound: 480
Since all of good you gain for me
Our common property shall be.
So whatever be the thing you with full conviction bring,
Let it now be boldly spoken: for our truce will not be broken.

Peithetaerus.

My mind, be sure, is eagerly at work, e'en now indeed
One ready-leaven'd argument the time is come to knead. 486
Ho, boy, a crown! and here, some slave, bring water quick, my hands to lave.

Euelpides.

Is there a dinner in the wind? or what are we to have?

477—80 (456—7). To which...expound (passed over by my witless mind: but this which you see speak publicly).

---

485 (462). Peithetaerus proceeds, by a comic induction, to demonstrate the ancient dignity and power of the Birds.

486 (463). A metaphor from the process of bread-making.

487 (463). As about to speak on a solemn occasion, Peithetaerus calls for a myrtle wreath and a ewer of water. Euelpides, pretending to mistake the motive, asks if they are going to dine.

Peithetaerus.

No: but I've long desired to speak a big well-fatten'd word,
By which the nation here may feel its spirit deeply stirr'd ; 490
So sorrowful am I for you, who anciently were kings.

Chorus.

We kings? of what?

Peithetaerus.

Indeed you were, of all existing things;
Of me, my friend here, Jove himself. Ere Kronos was, ye were;
Before the Titan brood and Earth.

Chorus.

And Earth?

Peithetaerus.

'Tis true, I swear. 494

Chorus.

I never heard, so help me Jove! a word of this before.

Peithetaerus.

You're such a dull incurious lot, unread in Aesop's lore;

---

490 (466). By which, &c. (which shall crush the soul of these).
494 (470). 'Tis true, I swear (yea by Apollo).

---

489 (465). "Well-fattened." The Greek word, usually applied to an ox, implies vastness and vigour.

493 (469). "Kronos" (Saturn), the mythic father of Zeus, is a name which suggests the remotest antiquity.

496 (471). "Aesop's lore." The life of Aesop (Aesopos), the renowned fabulist, is in a great degree legendary. He is said to have been a deformed Phrygian slave, about B.C. 570, contempo-

Whose story says, the lark was born first of the feathered
   quire,
Before the earth; then came a cold and carried off his
   sire:
Earth was not: five days lay the old bird untomb'd:
   at last the son
Buried the father in his head, since other grave was
   none. 500
            Euelpides.
The father of the lark lies dead, I understand, at Bury-
   head.
            Peithetaerus.
If then before the gods they were, and earlier than
   the earth,
Is not the kingdom theirs of right by eldership of
   birth?
            Euelpides.
True, by Apollo! so resolve henceforth a beak to rear:
The sceptre soon will Jove restore unto the woodpecker.

---

498 (473). Then came, &c. (and then that his father died from disease).
499 (474). Lay the old bird untombed (he was lying out).
500 (475). Since other grave was none (perplexed by helplessness).

---

rary with Solon and the seven sages. Fables of various countries
and authors are included in the collections which from ancient
times have been edited under the now familiar name of Aesop.

500 (475). "In his head." Theocritus (VII. 23), having in mind
this fable, calls larks 'tomb-crested.'

501 (476). "Bury-head;" lit. at Kephalai (heads), a borough of
the tribe Akamantis in Attica.

505 (480). The old reading here gives, 'Jove will *not* soon
restore, &c.' If this is right, the nurture of a beak is suggested
with a belligerent view. Commentators give reasons why the

Peithetaerus.

There's ample proof that birds, not gods, of yore were
    lords of men   506
And kings: first I'll produce the cock, who ruled the
    Persians then,
Ere aught was of Darius or of Megabazus heard;
And still, from that archaic rule, he's called the Persian
    bird.

Euelpides.

Like the great king he therefore struts, and on his
    head, full-drest,   510
Alone of all the birds he wears erect the turban-crest.

Peithetaerus.

So strong was he, so mighty then, so big, that to this
    hour,
When he his matin alto sings, in memory of that pow'r,
Smiths, potters, tanners, cordwainers, tradesfolk of every
    guild,
Cornfactors, bathing men, and such as frame the lyre
    and shield,   515

507—8 (482—3). Who ruled, &c. (who was sovereign and ruler of Persians before every Darius and Megabazus).

woodpecker is selected here: but these seem more fanciful than certain.

508 (484). No king called Megabazus ever reigned in Persia: but the name is that of a great family.

511 (487). "Turban-crest:" Gr. 'kurbasia;' also called 'tiara.' This erect crest was a privilege of the Persian monarch, whom Greek writers call 'the great king.'

513 (489). "Matin alto." The Greek means 'song of dawn,' but, one letter being removed, it expresses 'an alto strain.'

Spring up to work: some get them drest, ere night is
  o'er to start.
Euelpides.
Ask me to give that evidence: I know it to my
  smart;
I lost a cloak of Phrygian wool all through that bird,
  I did:
For, to a baby's naming-feast being in the city bid,
I drank a rouse and dozed awhile; then crew this cock
  ere yet   520
The rest had supped: I surely thought 'twas morn, and
  off I set
To Halimus; but scarce I'd poked my nose beyond the
  wall,

---

516 (492). "Get them drest:" lit. '*put on their shoes.*' Kock, approved by Meineke, advocates an emendation which gives the sense: 'others start in the night to steal cloaks.' But the starting in the night seems rather to point to the conduct of Euelpides, here described, than to that of the cloak-marauders. On the cock's crowing sometimes at evening, see *The Wasps*, v. 100.

518 (498). "Phrygian wool." Near Laodikea in Phrygia the sheep produced the finest wool. Hence the cloths of Miletus and other Asiatic towns were famous.

519 (499). "Naming-feast:" lit. 'tenth *day*.' The tenth day after birth was that on which the child received his name and recognition from the father. See v. 322.

520. "Drank a rouse." Euelpides came from his deme (Halimus) in the forenoon, and caroused before the evening meal (deipnon) which implies a late dinner or early supper. Hence becoming drowsy, he went to sleep, and, awakened by an evening cock-crow, started home as if morning were at hand.

522 (496). "Halimus," a deme of the tribe Leontis, thirty-five furlongs from Athens, near the harbour of Phaleron.

A footpad's bludgeon smote my back, I fell and tried
    to bawl:
But, ere I could so much as moan, my cloak was slipt,
    my robber flown.

Peithetaerus.

Ay, and a kite was ruling then the Hellenes, and was
    king.   525

Chorus.

The Hellenes?

Peithetaerus.

    Yes; and in his reign it first became the thing
To drop a reverence to the kites.

Euelpides.

    By Bacchus! 'twas my fate,
Spying a kite, to make my bow: then, tossing back
    my pate,
Down the red lane my money went, and I was forc'd
    to drag

---

524 (498). But, &c. (but he slipt off my cloak). 528—30 (502—3). Then, tossing, &c. (and then when throwing my head back I opened my mouth, I swallowed down the obol, and so dragged home the bag empty).

---

524 (497). The malpractices of cloak-stealing footpads are often mentioned. Orestes twice appears in this play as a notorious cloak-thief (lopodutes).

527 (501). "To the kites." The Athenians regarded kites as migratory birds (though not such), whose return announced summer earlier than that of the swallows. See the first Parabasis. Hence it was customary to salute the first seen kite.

529 (503). "My money:" lit. 'obol.' To carry small silver coins in the mouth seems to have been usual. See *The Wasps*, v. 609, 789. *Eccles.* 818.

Back to my home, all supperless and sad, an empty
   bag.   530
Peithetaerus.

In Egypt and Phoenike too a cuckoo fill'd the throne;
And when the cuckoo cried 'Cuckoo!' Phoenicians every
   one
The wheat and barley in the fields would reap with
   might and main.

Euelpides.

Ay truly, thence the saw, 'Cuckoo! ye cripples, to the
   plain.'
Peithetaerus.

So mighty was their sway that if in some Hellenic
   town   535
A king, as Agamemnon or his brother, wore the
   crown,
A bird upon their sceptres sat, the many bribes to
   share.

---

531 (504). Fill'd the throne (was king).
533 (506). Would reap with might and main (would reap).
536 (509). His brother (Menelaus). Wore the crown (reigned).

---

534 (507). "Ye cripples." The allusion here is to the practice of circumcision. The proverb resembles one cited by Suidas: 'Out of doors, ye Karians, the Anthesteria are ended:' *i.e.* 'Go to work; the holidays are over.'

537 (510). "Upon their sceptres." Herodotus (I. 195) speaks of images on sceptres (among them the eagle), as used by the Babylonians. In Homer the sceptre is the symbol of kingly power and rank.

"Bribes." To give rich presents to royal persons has been a custom prevalent in all ages, especially throughout the East.

Euelpides.

Well, this I never heard before: so I could only stare
When in the tragedies came forth some Priam, bird in
 hand,
That stood near base Lysikrates, and all his bribery
 scann'd.   540

Peithetaerus.

What strikes me most, the present Zeus a bird, an
 eagle, wears
Upon his statue's head, as king: an owl his daughter
 bears:
Apollo has a little hawk, as a mere serving-man.

Euelpides.

Right, by Demeter! and now what's the reason of the
 plan?

---

538 (511). I could only stare (wonder seized me).
541 (514). The present Zeus (Zeus who now reigns).
541—2 (515). Wears upon his statue's head (stands having on his head).

---

540 (513). "Lysikrates." No particulars of this person's corruption are known, though he is again mentioned by Aristophanes, *Eccles.* 630, 736.

542, &c. (515, &c.). The Greek in this passage would imply that not only Zeus, but also Pallas and Apollo, have a bird *on the head* of their statues; unless by a kind of zeugma, the word 'carries' alone is to be supplied as predicate of the two latter deities. The passage is difficult. Birds on sceptres are familiar (see Pind. *Pyth.* I. 10. Paus. v. 11): but on the heads of statues we hear of them nowhere else: nor does this position seem to favour the seizure of entrails offered to 'the hand.' Again, it is hard to understand why Apollo, carrying the hawk, is likened to a 'serving-man.' We can solve these difficulties only by saying that here, as indeed throughout the discourse of Peithetaerus, comic facts are perhaps invented to support a comic logic.

Peithetaerus.
That, when a sacrificer puts, according to our use,
The entrails in the hand, these birds may take them
 before Zeus. 546
No man would then swear by a god, but all men by
 the birds,
And Lampon still adjures the goose to back his cheat-
 ing words.—
Once, you see, you were high in place,
Once a great and a holy race, 550
Holy and great by all men deem'd,

549—52 (522—3). Once, you see, &c. (so great and holy did all formerly esteem you, but now on the other hand slaves).

---

546 (519). The translation here, "these birds," adopts a conjecture giving the pronoun 'these' instead of the common reading 'themselves,' from which it is impossible to extract any good meaning. See Note in Appendix. The whole passage still remains difficult, if any logical sequence is to be looked for. But perhaps Aristophanes lets Peithetaerus mystify 'the dull incurious lot' whom he addresses, by shewing a certain connexion between birds and deities, which results, somehow or other, in such an advantage to the birds, that they are enabled even to feast on dainties prepared for the Sire of gods and men.

548 (521). Lampon was a well-known soothsayer of the time, mentioned again at v. 988 and in *the Clouds*, 332. He signed the Treaties with Lakedaemon. See Thuk. v. 19.

"The goose." Swearing by animals and trees was a curious ancient practice, intended, as we are told, to avoid the irreverent mention of deities in ordinary conversation. Besides the goose we find the dog, the ram, the plane-tree thus invoked. Becker suggests that 'chena,' *the goose*, was substituted for 'Zena,' *Jove*. Such quasi-reverent substitutions are frequent enough in the parlance of several modern languages, as English, French, German.

Now as the merest jacks esteem'd.
If in their temples you now alight,
They pelt you like any bedlamite:
And the cunning fowlers for you set   555
Snare and springe, twig, trap, gin, cage and net:
Then they catch and sell you by the score,
And the buyers feel and pinch you sore:
Till, at last, when comes the sad decree,
They don't even roast you decently;   560
But the grated cheese they first prepare,
Adding silphium, oil and vinegar,
And they rub in these with cruel care:
Then a sauce they heat that's rich and sweet,
And drench you with it, like dry dog's meat.   565

Chorus.

By far, O man, alas! by far   *Antistrophe.*
These tales of all most cruel are
Which to mine ears you bring,
And from me tears you wring
For those my coward sires, who could   570
Thus in my babyhood

---

559 (531). When comes the sad decree (if it is resolved to do this).

---

552 (523). "Jacks:" Gr. 'Manas.' Manes was an ordinary slave's name.'

566, &c. (539, &c.). The Birds regret their lost dominion, and desire the counsel of Peithetaerus about the means of recovering it.

571 (543). "In my babyhood." Another reading would express 'to my damage.'

Abandon mighty privileges
Sent down from old ancestral ages.
But, as you're come by heaven's decree
And happy chance a saviour unto me,   575
My nestlings and myself I give
In your protectorate to live.
Forthwith then teach us what to do: since life's not
    worth the name,
Unless by fair means or by foul our kingdom we re-
    claim.

Peithetaerus.

First then I teach that of the birds one city you shall
    found,   580
And next that all this atmosphere that circles you
    around,
And all the ways that intervene the earth and sky
    between,
With huge baked bricks, like Babylon, be walled about
    by you.

Euelpides.

O Gog and Magog, what a town! how terrible to view!

580, &c. (550, &c.). Peithetaerus develops his plan of restitution. The Birds must found an aerial city, between earth and heaven, wall out the gods, and declare themselves the rulers and benefactors of mankind. Euelpides chimes in with a series of ludicrous illustrations.

583 (552). The walls of Babylon, built by Semiramis of baked bricks, are said by Herodotus to have embraced a circuit of twelve geographical miles.

584 (553). "Gog and Magog:" Gr. 'Kebriones and Porphyrion.' These were two of the giants.

Peithetaerus.

When this has gain'd its perfect height, reclaim from
    Zeus the sway: 585
And if he won't knock under straight, but still returns
    a 'Nay,'
Announce to him a sacred war, and notify the gods
They must not pass, as heretofore, through your
    august abodes
A courting of their Semeles, Alkmenas and the rest:
Such contraband amours shall now most strictly be
    supprest. 590
To men you'll also send a bird as herald with these
    words:
'Henceforth, as birds are reigning, you must sacrifice
    to birds,
And to the gods in second rank: whereto must be
    assign'd
For every god a proper bird, the fittest you can find.
Aphrodite's sacrifice crumpets for the coot implies;
If a sheep Poseidon gain, wheat-corn let the duck
    obtain; 596
Comes for Herakles a treat? honey-cakes the gull must
    eat;
If king Zeus a ram delight, we've our kingbird, who,
    by right,

---

587 (556). "A sacred war." The wars concerning the temple at Delphi were called by the Greeks 'sacred wars.' Of these the earliest is that mentioned in Thuk. I. 112.

598 (568). "Kingbird," Gr. 'orchilos,' a small wren, so called. The smallness of the bird makes the comparison more comic.

Zeus himself preceding, can claim a slaughter'd gnat
  from man.'
                    Euelpides.
Slaughter'd gnat! charming that! let him thunder now,
  great Zan!   600
                    Chorus.
But how shall we to human gaze appear as gods
  instead of jays,
Flying about and wearing wings?
                  Peithetaerus.
                           All nonsense! Hermes flies,
God as he is; and wings are worn by countless deities.
Lo, Victory soars on golden wings, and Eros too, by
  Jove,
And Hera likewise, Homer says, went like a trembling
  dove.   605
And, when it thunders, does not Zeus the winged
  lightning on us loose?
                    Chorus.
But if mere cyphers we shall seem to unenlightened
  men,
Olympians only count as gods?
                  Peithetaerus.
                           A cloud of sparrows then

---

600 (570). "Zan." The old Doric form for Zeus.

605 (575). "Hera." The common reading here gives 'Iris.' But the passage alluded to in the Iliad (v. 778) mentions Hera and Athene as 'moving like trembling doves.' Iris however, with Eileithuia, is cited with the same description in the Homeric Hymns (I. 114). Possibly therefore the reading 'Irin' may be right.

And grain-devourers off the land shall all their seed-
  corn eat;
Then let Demeter, when they starve, dole out to them
  her wheat. 610

Euelpides.

She never will, so help me Zeus! you'll see her making
  some excuse.

Peithetaerus.

Again the ravens may tear out, if thus it must be tried,
The eyes of all their ploughing kine and all their sheep
  beside:
Then let Apollo heal, if he's as rich in science as in
  fees.

Euelpides.

Pray, till I've sold my little team of bullocks twain,
  don't try the scheme. 615

Peithetaerus.

But, if they deem you god, you life, you earth, you
  Kronos, you
Poseidon, they shall have all goods.

Chorus.

　　　　　Just mention one or two.

---

610 (580). "Dole out:" as rich people to the poor in times of dearth. Demeter (Ceres), the goddess of corn and harvest.

612 (583). "If thus it must be tried." So Kock. Or possibly, 'This is worth being tried.'

614 (584). Lit. 'Let Apollo heal, being a physician: he takes fees.' Apollo was a healing as well as a prophetic deity. His 'taking fees' is an allusion to the great wealth and rich ornaments presented or deposited in his temples.

Peithetaerus.

First, locusts shall not feed upon their vine-shoots: but this pest
Shall by a single troop of owls and falcons be supprest:
Next, on their figs at no time shall the nits and maggots prey; 620
One flight of thrushes shall pick out and clear them all away.

Chorus.

But wealth, which men so dearly love, whence are we to bestow?

Peithetaerus.

When they consult, these birds to them the paying mines will shew,
And all the profitable marts they'll mention to the seer,
So that no captain will be lost.

Chorus.

None lost? Let that appear. 625

Peithetaerus.

When about sailing men consult, some bird will still explain,
'Don't sail at present, there'll be storm: sail now, 'tis certain gain.'

---

623 (593). "Consult:" i.e. the oracles. Cobet's conjecture ('ta men alla' for 'ta metalla') removes the mention of mines, supplying this sense: 'to men when they consult, these birds, besides giving all good things, will also mention,' &c. This is highly ingenious, but cannot be regarded as certainly true.

Euelpides.

A bark I buy, command a crew: I won't stay daw-
dling here with you.

Peithetaerus.

They'll shew them too the hidden coins which men of
old laid down:
They know them all: a saying 'tis familiar to the
town:— 630
My treasure, where it lies interr'd, none knows, unless
it be some bird.

Euelpides.

I sell my bark, a spade I buy, and grubbing up the
gutters try.

Chorus.

But how are we to give them Health, which with the
gods doth dwell?

Peithetaerus.

Good Fortune—is not that good Health?

Euelpides.

Yes, all the world can tell,
When a man's doing very ill, he can't be very well.

Chorus.

But how shall they attain old age, a pure Olympian
privilege? 636
Must they decease in childhood?

---

635 (605). "Doing ill." This literally renders the Greek phrase, which, like the English, ordinarily means 'unfortunate,' 'in bad circumstances,' and yet is ambiguous enough to support the intended play of words.

Peithetaerus.

      No, by Jove! dismiss your fears:
They'll get a bonus from the birds of full three hundred years.

Chorus.

Who'll give them to the birds?

Peithetaerus.

      Who give? themselves: why, don't you know,
'Five generations of mankind exists the chattering
    crow'?   640

Euelpides.

Hurrah! hurrah! better by far
Than Zeus for us these bird-kings are.

Peithetaerus.

True indeed: for there'll be no need
Temples of stone for these to rear:
Golden doors will be useless gear;   645
Under the holms and holly trees
They'll be hopping and dwelling at ease:
Place for the statelier birds we'll find
In the boughs of an olive shrined.
Unto Delphi or Ammon's fane   650
Carrying victims will be vain:

637—8 (607—8). No, by Jove, &c. (no, by Jove! but the birds will add to them three hundred years more).

---

640 (609). This line is from Hésiod, *Op. et D.* 747.

650 (619). "Ammon's fane." The temple of Jupiter Ammon was in Egypt.

If in arbute and olive shade
Plates of barley and wheat be laid,
Stretching our hands we'll ask in pray'r
Of their blessings an ample share: 655
All we seek we are sure to gain
Just for tossing a little grain.

Chorus.

Old man, of late my bitterest foe, but now my dearest friend,
Your guidance will I nevermore forsake unto the end.
Elated by your words I swear, 660
And threateningly declare,
If you will covenant on your part
With just, sincere, religious heart,
To march against the gods, with me
Allied in perfect harmony, 665
Not very long the powers divine
Shall grasp the sceptre that is mine.
All the work, where strength is needed, be to us assign'd,
While to you shall be committed all requiring mind.

Hoopoe.

Now, let me tell you, there's no further time 670

658—9 (626—7). Old man, &c. (far dearest to me of old men, becoming so from the most odious, it cannot be that I shall ever again wilfully depart from your opinion).

---

658 (626), &c. The Birds gratefully accept the counsel of Peithetaerus, and desire his alliance in 'a war against the gods.'

670 (638), &c. The hoopoe invites the Athenians to enter his

To nod and shilly-shally, Nikias-like;
But something must be done forthwith. First enter
And view my nest, my straws and stock of firewood:
And let us know your names.

Peithetaerus.
An easy matter.
My name is Peithetaerus, and my friend's   675
Euelpides of Krio.

Hoopoe.
Welcome both.

Peithetaerus.
We thank you.

Hoopoe.
Enter in then.

Peithetaerus.
Certainly.
Pray take and introduce us.

Hoopoe.
Forward, then.

Peithetaerus.
Yet something strikes me: just come back awhile,

---

dwelling, and inquires their names. He promises to supply them with a certain root, by eating which they will acquire wings.

671 (639). "Shilly-shally, Nikias-like." This is expressed by one Greek word, coined for the occasion. The allusion is to the general character of Nikias, but especially to the hesitating scruples and difficulties raised by him in the Athenian assembly to impede the Sicilian expedition. See Thuk. VI. 25.

676 (645). Krio or Krioa was a deme of the tribe Antiochis.

679 (648). "Something strikes me." This renders the very

Let's see: please tell us, how will he and I,   680
Non-flyers, live on terms with you that fly?

Hoopoe.

Quite well.

Peithetaerus.

     Nay, pause awhile. In Aesop's fables
There is an ancient story of the fox,
How bad a lodger once it found the eagle.

Hoopoe.

Pluck up your spirits: there's a certain root,   685
Which when you've eaten, you'll at once have wings.

Peithetaerus.

Then let us enter in. Ho, Xanthias
And Manodorus, take the baggage up.

Chorus.

Sir, with you a word or two!

Hoopoe.

     What?

Chorus.

     Let these men lunch with you
Bravely: but the musical, most melodious nightingale
Summon forth, and let her stay here awhile, with us
    to play.   691

---

peculiar Greek phrase (to deina) in the sense which is found to belong to it in use.

   683 (652). "The fox." The fox in the fable, whose hole was at the foot of the tree, could not pursue the eagle which carried off her cubs to its eyrie at the summit.

   689 (658). The Chorus of Birds request the hoopoe to call the nightingale out of the brake, and leave her with them to sing

Peithetaerus.
Pray, Sir, refuse not: speak a friendly word,
And from the rushbrake fetch the little bird.
Euelpides.
Yes, bring her hither: let our suit prevail,
That we too may behold the nightingale. 695
Hoopoe.
If both desire, I must: out, Prokne dear,
And be presented to the strangers here.

The Nightingale *enters from the bush.*
Peithetaerus.
Wide-honour'd Zeus! a charming birdie this,
So beautiful, so fair, so tender 'tis,
And wearing heaps of gold, like some young Miss. 700
Euelpides.
I want to kiss her.
Peithetaerus.
That's a maddish freak:
She's got a pair of scissors for a beak.
Euelpides.
But from her noddle I could peel the shell,
As from an egg, and kiss her very well.

---

and play, while he entertains the Athenians at luncheon. The visitors, desiring to see her, second the motion. Prokne comes out, drest as a female fluteplayer, with a mouthpiece and many golden ornaments, exciting the admiration of the two friends. They retire into the bush with the hoopoe, who now disappears from the action of the play, Peithetaerus having accepted the future presidency of the feathered commonwealth.

703 (673). "Peel the shell:" i.e. 'take off the mouthpiece.'

Hoopoe.

Come, let's be moving.

Peithetaerus.

    Lead the way, my friend, 705
And may good fortune still our steps attend.

 [*Exeunt Hoopoe, Peithetaerus, Euelpides, and Slaves.*

 [*The Chorus chant or intone the first Parabasis.*

    (*Kommation.*)

O my ownie, O my brownie,
 Bird of birds the dearest,
Voice that mingling with my lays
 Ever was the clearest,   710
Playmate of my early days,
 Still to me the nearest,

707—839 (676—800). Here follows the first Parabasis, or central portion of the old Greek Comedy, in which the Chorus wheels round towards the spectators, and addresses to them a chant or rather a series of chants, complete in this Comedy. First comes the 'kommation,' or short lyric introduction, here a vernal greeting to the nightingale, who, as a flutist, is invited to perform a symphony. After this follows the Parabasis proper, usually in the long anapaestic measure, the subject having some relation to the plot of the piece, often to the author himself. It concludes with a shorter anapaestic system, called 'makron' or 'pnigos,' which see at v. 762 (723). Then follows an 'ode' of a poetic character, and a recitative of (usually) sixteen burlesque verses, called 'epirrhema.' To these correspond severally the 'antode' and 'antepirrhema,' concluding the whole Parabasis. This play has a second Parabasis at v. 1127 (1058), which consists only of ode and epirrhema, with antode and antepirrhema.

Nightingale, thus again
Do I meet thee, do I greet thee,
Bringing to me thy sweet strain? 715
  Skilfullest of artists thou
To soft trillings of the flute
Vernal melodies to suit,
  Our homily demands thy prelude now.
    [*The Nightingale plays a flute symphony.*
    (*Parabasis* **proper**.)
Ho! ye men dim-lived by nature, closest to the leaves
  in feature, 720
Feeble beings, clay-create, shadowy tribes inanimate,
Wingless mortals, in a day, doleful, dreamlike, swept
  away;
Note the lessons that we give, we the immortals form'd
  to live,
We the ethereal, the unaged, with undying plans engaged:

---

719 (684). "Our homily:" lit. '*anapaests.*' The translation is not anapaestic, but trochaic: an anapaestic version being added in the appendix. This Parabasis is an evident parody of the mythic genealogies in the Orphic Hymns, which were dressed up to please the popular ear in the lectures of the rhetorical sophists. It appears from v. 728 (692) that Aristophanes in this Ornithogony specially ridicules the lectures of Prodikus. That sophist, a native of the isle of Keos, taught at Athens for about forty years. He applied himself especially to the critical distinction of words, and to mythic and allegorical narration. His chief work was entitled *Horae*, and in it was contained the Choice of Herakles, that famous apologue quoted by Xenophon in his *Memorabilia of Sokrates*, II. 1. 21, and called by Cicero, 'Hercules Prodiceus.'

720 (685). "The leaves:" an allusion to Hom. *Il.* VI. 146: 'such as the race of leaves is that of men.'

That, when ye have heard aright all our lore of highest
    flight,   725
Birds and what their true creation, gods and what
    their generation,
All the rivers running through Erebus and Chaos too,
Ye may cry, well train'd by us, 'What care we for
    Prodikus?'
Chaos was and Night of yore in the time all times
    before,
And black Erebus beside Tartarus extending wide.
Earth, Air, Heaven were yet unknown, in huge Erebus
    alone   731
First, our oldest legend says, black-wing'd Night a
    wind-egg lays;
Which, as circling seasons move, brings to birth the
    charmer Love,
Bright with golden wings behind, semblant to the whirl-
    ing wind.
In the vast Tartarean shade him the dull dark Chaos
    made   735
Sire of us: we nestled there till we saw the light of
    air.
Race immortal there was none till Love's sorcery was
    begun:
But, when all things mixed in motion, rose the sky,
    the earth, the ocean,
And the blessèd gods were made, everlasting, unde-
    cay'd.
Thus of all the blessèd we far the oldest claim to be;
And that we are sons of Love many facts agree to
    prove: 741

Still we fly our daily round, still with lovers we are
    found :
Cruel hearts will oft relent if a pretty bird is sent ;
And a quail, or goose, or dove, wins the victory for
    Love.
Of the goods with which they're blest mortals get from
    birds the best.   745
First, of seasons, winter, spring, summer, we the tokens
    bring.
Men must sow, when shrieks the crane seeking Libya's
    coast again ;
That's the time, each captain knows, to hang up the
    helm and doze :
Then Orestes must not lack cloak well-woven for his
    back,
Lest with cold the robber freeze and another's garment
    seize.   750
Next the kite appears, and brings a new season on
    his wings,
When the flock you must release from its vernal load
    of fleece.
Then the swallow comes to tell time is come the cloak
    to sell,
And, for wear while days are hot, buy the slender
    paletot.
We are Ammon's shrine to you, Delphi and Dodona
    too,   755

---

749 (712). "Orestes :" the footpad and cloak-robber; see v. 523 (497).

Phoebus' self: to birds you turn first, whatever you
    would learn,
How to choose a mart, a trade, or a marriageable
    maid.
The decisive omens all known in seercraft, birds you
    call;
Bird an oracle of fate, bird a sneeze you designate:
Sign that's seen or voice that's heard, lacquey, donkey,
    'tis a bird.   760
We're Apollo then, 'tis clear; we're your only Pythian
    seer.
So then, if for gods you take us,
And your trusted muse-seers make us,
Gentle breezes we will send you;
Pleasant seasons shall attend you;   765
Moderate heat when summer's nearest,
Moderate cold when winter's drearest:
We'll not sulk, and sit beclouded
High in Jove-like grandeur shrouded;
But, in lower ether gliding,   770
Near your mansions still abiding,
We will give to all your nations,
Through their latest generations,

---

758 (719). "Birds you call." Ancient superstition divined the future (1) from the flight and cries of birds (augury), (2) from voices and oracles, (3) from wayside objects and occurrences (sumbola), (4) from observation of sacrifices. See Xen. *Mem.* I. 1. 3, Aesch. *Prom.* 485, Theophr. *Char.* 25, Hor. *C.* III. 27. Any omen was familiarly called 'a bird:' whence the comic poet in this place draws his witticism.

Life that's healthy, peace that's wealthy,
Youth-enhancing feast and dancing,   775
And, with laughter, bird's milk after.
All shall say, ' 'Tis really cloying :'
Such the bliss you'll be enjoying.

(Ode.)

Muse of the woodland glade,
    Tio, tio, tio, tio, tio, tio, tiotix,   780
Harmonist, whom tending oft
In glens or on the mountain tops aloft,
    Tio, tio, tio, tiotix,
Perch'd in an ash-tree's leafy shade,
    Tio, tio, tio, tiotix,   785
Through my brown bill to Pan I raise
Melodious strains of holy praise,
And to the mountain Mother solemn choral lays.
    Totototototototototix.

---

776 (734). "Bird's milk," which here crowns the list of blessings promised by the Birds, is often jocularly cited as a fabulous dainty. So Plin. N. H. Praef. 'Vel lactis gallinacei sperare haustum.' The translator recollects from early days the practical joke of sending a child to buy a pennyworth of 'pigeon's milk.'

779 (737). The choric odes of comedy are often imitations of those in tragedy, fragments of which are here and there borrowed and interwoven, so as to form an amusing parody of a style so familiar to the Athenian public from the annual tragic contests. This purpose is obvious enough in this ode; but still more so in the antode at v. 809 (769). The lyrics of the old tragic poet Phrynichus were always popular (see *The Wasps*, v. 220, 269), and are probably parodied here by Aristophanes. See v. 790 (750).

788 (746). "The mountain Mother:" i.e. the goddess Kybelē, great Mother of the Gods, worshipped in the mountains and woods

Whence, beelike, Phrynichus his soul did fill 790
With fruit of melodies ambrosial, still
Carolling lyrics at his own sweet will.

(*Epirrhema.*)

Sirs, if any of your throng to the bird-club will belong,
We can offer him a home full of bliss for years to come.
What your laws entitle base, what you visit with disgrace, 795
We the birds commend and deem worthy of our high esteem.
Here by law 'tis very bad if a youngster beats his dad:
There with us 'tis usual rather, even grand, to cuff a father,
Strutting up and crying, 'Sir, if you'll fight me, lift your spur.' 799
Any of you that has been branded for a runaway,
As a speckled francolin may with us securely stay.
Any half-caste Spintharus, from the land of bamboos,
Blackbird will be call'd by us, cousin of our Sambos.

---

of Phrygia, and constantly associated with Pan, as in Pind. *Pyth.* III. 78, *Fragm.* 71.

793 (753), &c. Come to us birds, says the Chorus in the epirrhema, all ye Athenians who find your own laws and customs too strict and too moral; we will give you a hearty welcome and all the licence you can wish. The Chorus, when addressing the spectators, localizes itself among them: *here* means at Athens, *there* means in Bird-land: while in the scenic parts the converse is true.

800 (760). Runaway slaves were often branded when taken.

802 (762). Spintharus was a poor tragic poet, represented here as of mixed blood. Lit. *If any one is a Phrygian* (barbarian) *like Spintharus, he shall be a 'phrugilos'* (unknown bird), *of*

If, like Exekestides, some vile Karian slave comes out,
Pappies he can fledge with ease there, and wardsmen
    soon will sprout.   805
To the outlaws would some day Peisias' son the gates
    betray?
He, true nestling of his sire, partridge-rank can there
    acquire:
Sneaking out we reckon fair, partridge-fashion, from
    the snare.

Philemon's family (unknown).' Liberty has been taken to make the half-caste a mulatto, the bird a blackbird, and Philemon Sambo. If the comic poet may dare *anything* for the sake of humour, his translator must occasionally dare *something*, lest the humour evaporate altogether.

804—5 (764—5). Lit. *If any one is a Karian slave, as Exekestides* (see v. 11), *let him fledge 'pappoi' with us, and 'phrateres' will appear.* 'Pappos' means a grandsire, and also the down on the seeds of certain flowers, as the dandelion. The 'phrateres' are the members of the ward or 'phratria,' to whom a child was presented by his father, in order to be registered in their list as an Athenian citizen. In this place the 'pappoi' represent the downy pinfeathers of a young bird, and the 'phrateres' represent the plumes or full-grown feathers. What is conveyed by the whole passage is: that a spurious claimant of the suffrage, producing a crop of ancestors, will find wardsmen lax enough to enroll him on their list.

806 (766). The son of Peisias is one Meles, a musician (kitharōdos), father of the dithyrambic poet Kinesias, afterwards introduced. Of the treasons here imputed to Meles and Peisias there is no other record. The outlaws probably mean those who fled on account of the prosecution of the Hermokopidae. The partridge is said by Aristotle and Pliny to draw the fowler away from its nest by pretending lameness (hence the verb used); but this is rather true of the lapwing. An allusion is supposed to the wavering policy of Perdikkas king of Makedonia.

(*Antode.*)
So swans in olden tide,
    Tio, tio, tio, tio, tio, tio, tiotix,   810
Did their trilling pinions poise
And chant Apollo with commingling noise,
    Tio, tio, tio, tiotix,
Perch'd on a knoll by Hebrus' side,
    Tio, tio, tio, tiotix.   815
Came through the airy cloud a cry,
The dappled wild-beasts crouching lie,
And sinks the billowy sea beneath the windless sky.
    Totototototototototix.
Olympus echoed to his utmost bound,   820
Amazement seiz'd the kings, and far around
Each Grace and Muse Olympian swell'd the sound.
    Tio, tio, tio, tiotix.

(*Antepirrhema.*)
Of all joys and blessings none beats the having feathers on.
One of you spectators may, wearing wings at any play,   825
Get at last a peckish feel, and desire a quiet meal:
Home he'll fly, just take a snack, then, with belly full, fly back.
Any other small affair, wanting only speed and care,
Flying helps you to get through quietly and quickly too.
Flying oft with full success crowns a lover's happiness.

824—39 (785—800). Wings, says the Chorus, are the most handy things imaginable. Comic instances of their convenience are adduced. Some of the lines here are not literally translated.

If he spies his rival here in the senatorial tier, 831
He can spread his wings and fly, love-directed, through
 the sky,
Keep his happy tryst, and then fly into his seat again.
Isn't it then the best of things to possess a pair of
 wings?
In Dieitrephes we find proof enough for any mind:
Osier wings were all his claim, yet a captain he be-
 came 836
By his tribesmen duly voted, thence to higher grade
 promoted;

---

831 (794). "The senatorial tier." The Senate (boulê) of 500 had special seats in the theatre.

835—9 (798—800). Lit. '*since Dieitrephes, having osier wings only, was chosen phularch, then hipparch, and so from being nobody he has a great fortune, and is now a brown horsecock.*' This person had become rich by the manufacture of wicker wine-flasks, called here 'osier wings.' He was elected first one of the ten phularchs (captains of the cavalry of the ten tribes), then one of the two hipparchs (colonels of cavalry), whence he is jestingly called Horsecock. 'Horse' in compounds implies bigness; and this term, taken from Aeschylus, is again cited in *The Frogs*, v. 932—7, where it is explained as a figure-head of a ship. The simile is meant to describe a tall strutting officer of cavalry in brown uniform; and, from v. 1530 (1442), we also find that this Dieitrephes was fond of horse-driving. Elmsley receives the form Dieitrephes from an ancient marble. Probably he is the same Diitrephes who lost his life in the following year, B.C. 413. He escorted back to Thrace a body of mercenaries who arrived too late to sail with Demosthenes to Syracuse. These barbarians landed in Boeotia, captured the town of Mykalessus, and massacred the inhabitants; but were then defeated and pursued to their ships with great slaughter by the Thebans; Diitrephes himself receiving a mortal wound. See Thuk. VII. 29; Grote's *Hist.* II. lxi.

Now he gives himself grand airs, once the roughest of
  the roughs,
And the title that he bears, Colonel Horsecock of the
  Buffs.

Enter PEITHETAERUS *and* EUELPIDES *as birds.*

Peithetaerus.

So far so good. No, never, on my word,   840
I never saw a creature more absurd.

Euelpides.

What are you laughing at?

Peithetaerus.

                     Oh, don't you know?
Those pin-feathers of yours amuse me so.
Such metamorphosis your wings produce,
You're very like a cheaply-painted goose.   845

Euelpides.

You've limn'd my likeness: yours is quite as droll,
A blackbird stript of feathers round the poll.

   842—3 (803—4). Oh, &c. (at your pinfeathers: do you know what you are most like, having wings?)
   846—7 (805). You've, &c. (and you to a blackbird plucked about the poll).

---

   840 (801), &c. The two Athenians reenter, wearing grotesque birdmasks and plumage. After mutual banter they proceed to discuss, with the Chorus, the name and arrangements of the new city. Here begins the Second Episode.

Peithetaerus.

These likenesses we get—the poet sings—
Wrought of none other, but by our own wings.

Chorus.

What's the next business?

Peithetaerus.

We are bound to frame,
First thing of all, a great and glorious name   851
For our new city. Sacrifice is due,
Next, to the powers divine.

Euelpides.

I think so too.

Chorus.

What title for our city shall we choose?

Peithetaerus.

That which the folk at Lakedaemon use,   855
That big one, Sparta, would you give it?

848—9 (807—8). "The poet:" Aeschylus, who in a lost play, cites a Libyan fable of the eagle shot by an arrow feathered from its own wing. In the second line the words are those of Aeschylus. Peithetaerus jestingly means: 'these wings which enable us thus to banter each other, are of our own growing (by virtue of the root), not borrowed from any bird.'

854 (811), &c. The speeches here ascribed to Euelpides are those which seem to suit his character best. Holden assigns to the Chorus that in which a cloudy title is recommended: but it is noticeable that Peithetaerus replies with a verb in the second person singular, whereas he replied to the Chorus with the corresponding plural in v. 856 (813).

Euelpides.

         Fie!
Take for my city Sparta? No, not I:
The meanest pallet never should receive
So poor a fitting, while I'd girths to give.

Peithetaerus.

What must we call it then?

Euelpides.

        From this new home,
These nebulous altitudes in which we roam,   861
Some vaunting title take to suit it pat.

Peithetaerus.

Cloudcuckooborough,—what d'ye say to that?

Chorus.

Bravo! bravo! invention's quite your forte;
A very noble name and—not too short.   865

 856—9 (814—16). Fie...give (Herakles! should I join Sparte to my city? no not to a pallet bed, if I had any girths).
 860—3 (817—19). From this new home...that (from hence, from the clouds and elevated places, some very boastful one. Will you have Cloudcuckooborough?)
 865 (820). A very, &c. (the name you've invented is downright beautiful and large).

---

 857 (815). A plant called 'sparton' (a kind of broom) was used to make a cheap bed-rope, called 'Sparte,' here jestingly confounded with the city of the same name.
 863 (818). "Cloudcuckooborough:" Gr. 'Nephelokokkygia.' A city built on clouds and inhabited by cuckoos (regarded as vain birds) represents a mere unreality, a 'castle in the air.'

Euelpides.
Is this the same Cloudcuckooborough, pray,
In which Theogenes has stowed away
Most of his wealth, and Aeschines his all?

Peithetaerus.
Or, haply, Phlegra's plain 'twill best recall,
Where gods outshot the boastful giant foes   870
With louder-boasting braggadocios.

Euelpides.
A smartish city this! But who shall dwell,
As guardian godhead, in the citadel?

869—71 (823—5). Or, haply, &c. (and best of all indeed the plain of Phlegra, where the gods outshot the giants *in* vain-boasting).

---

867 (822). "Theogenes" was a man of some note at Athens. We find him in commission with Kleon at Sphakteria, see Thuk. IV. 27; and afterwards signing the treaties of peace: see Thuk. v. 19. 24. After the date of this play he was engaged in an embassy to the great king, and became one of the Thirty, B.C. 404. The comic poets ridicule him as a pompous pretender, and as uncleanly. See *The Peace*, v. 928.

868 (823). This "Aeschines," who was called 'the son of Sellus' (Sellus being a cant name for an ostentatious beggar), became one of the Thirty, and was sent on an embassy to Lakedaemon. See Xen. *Hell.* II. 3. 13. The wealth of Theogenes and Aeschines, having no real existence, is aptly placed in Cloudcuckooborough.

869 (824). The plain of "Phlegra," on which the fabulous battle was fought between the gods and giants, was assigned to various localities in Pallene, Asia, Italy, &c. Aristophanes places it, as an unreal legend, in the region of Cloudcuckooborough. It was a battle, he comically says, in which the victory was gained by those who 'drew the longest bow.'

873 (827). As the citadel of Athens (called Akropolis or Polis) had for its presiding deity Pallas Athenaea or Athene, with the

For whom the broidered mantle?

Peithetaerus.

       Can't we still
Let Athenaea keep the sacred hill?   875

Euelpides.

A wisely-ordered state can any be,
Where stands in highest shrine a deity
Female of sex, who, clad in armour, sees,
With shuttle in his hand, a Kleisthenes?

Peithetaerus.

To guard the Storkwall whom shall we engage? 880

874—5 (828). Can't we still, &c. (why leave we not Athenaea citadel-keeper?)
877—9 (830—1). Where stands...hand (where a deity, being woman, stands having a panoply, and Kleisthenes a shuttle?)

---

title Polias, Euelpides asks who shall preside in the citadel of Cloudcuckooborough? for whom shall a mantle (peplos) be woven like the splendidly embroidered robe carried in procession at the Panathenaea or great feast of Pallas Polias? Peithetaerus, as if forgetting he is not at Athens, suggests that Athenaea should remain in charge of the citadel. This leads up to the jest of Euelpides, who asks how a city can be well-conditioned in which a goddess stands (sculptured by Pheidias) in full armour, while a man, Kleisthenes, is of such effeminate habits, that a shuttle is his most appropriate symbol. On this Kleisthenes, an unmanly noble, see *The Knights*, v. 1374: *The Clouds*, v. 355: *Thesmophor.* v. 574, &c.

880 (832). "Storkwall:" Gr. 'Pelargic' (from 'pelargos,' a stork) or 'Pelasgic wall.' Aristophanes prefers the former name, which connects it with the birds. See again v. 922 (869). This wall, partly ruined in the Persian war, flanked the Athenian Akropolis, and is comically transferred to the Bird-citadel.

Chorus.
A bird of ours of Persian parentage,
Whose fear-awakening fame resounds afar,
The gallant chicken of the god of war,

Euelpides.
O my lord Chicken! ay, 'tis chosen well;
No god is fitter upon rocks to dwell. 885

Peithetaerus.
Now you start off, ascend the upper air,
And lend a hand to help the masons there:
Pass on the lime, to mix the mortar strip,
Carry the hod up, from the ladder slip;
Appoint the watch, the fire still hidden keep, 890
Run round the beat with bell, there fall asleep.
Despatch one herald to the gods on high,
To men beneath another from the sky;
For me returning bid him ask.

Euelpides.
I see;
You mean to rest here; rest and hang—for me. 895

---

883 (835). "God of war." Lukian reports a legend that a youth, placed as sentinel by the war-god Ares, neglected his duty, and was changed into a cock, a bird of martial aspect and temper. The cock is said to be a fear-awakening name everywhere, because, by his crowing, he compels many people to leave their beds unwillingly: and he is fit to dwell on rocks, as a sentinel whose signals should be heard as far as possible.

886 (837). Euelpides, whose blunt comic criticisms are no longer needed, is now dismissed, and does not reappear. The directions given to him by Peithetaerus mix the ludicrous with the serious.

894—5 (845—6). As if offended by some of the directions, Euelpides, instead of saying 'good bye,' says 'stay and be hanged

Peithetaerus.

Go on your mission, friend: without you none
Of all the things I mention will be done.
         [*Exit Euelpides.*
Now must we hold a solemn sacrifice
In honour of the new-made deities;
And I will fetch a priest to range the show.   900
Lads, lift the basket and the ewer. So.
         [*Exit Peithetaerus.*

Chorus.

I say so too: I vote with you,   *Strophe.*
Yes, and add one counsel due:
To the gods devout profession
Let us make in grand procession,   905
And, to win their favour, bring
A nice sheep as offering.
Utter forth, utter high
To the god a Pythian cry;
And let Chaeris to our lay   910
Flauto obligato play.

A Fluteplayer, *wearing the mask of a raven with a mouthpiece, enters and begins to play.*

---

for me,' parodying the 'for me' used in another sense by Peithetaerus.

 899 (848). "The new-made deities." See v. 594 (564).

 902 (851). While Peithetaerus is away, the Chorus chant a short Chorikon (of which the Antistrophe is at v. 945 (895)), and call in a fluteplayer.

 910 (858). "Chaeris," ridiculed by Aristophanes as a bad fluteplayer. See *Acharn.* 16. 866.

 915 (861). "Mouthpiece," Gr. 'phorbeia.' This was a kind of

Enter PEITHETAERUS *with* a Priest.

Peithetaerus.

A truce there to your puffing! Herakles!
What creature's this? Will marvels never cease?
Full many a wondrous sight I've seen, but none
To match a raven with a mouthpiece on.   915
Your office now begins; initiate, priest,
To the new gods our sacrificial feast.

Priest.

I'll do the solemn duty, since you ask it:
But where is he that bears the sacred basket?
Let us pray to Hestia birdqueen of flame; and to
the holy Kite that guards the same—   921

---

leathern respirator fastened round his jaws by the flute-player to moderate the effusion of his breath in playing.

920—39 (865—86). In this passage the style and dialect of the ancient Ionic liturgies are parodied, and their prose form kept. The new bird-deities are comically associated with the old; but to Hestia (Vesta) the first cited, no bird-name is assigned. She could not be omitted, being the goddess of the hearth, who maintained the holy fire in house, ward-room, and townhall. The kite takes the place of the hearth-keeping Zeus. The swan represents Apollo of Delphi and Delos, the 'ortugometra' (mother-quail) Lato; the goldfinch (akalanthis) is Artemis; the 'phrugilos' is the mysterious Sabazian Dionysus of Phrygia; the sparrow (or ostrich?) is the Great Mother Kybele. To these are joined a number of hero-birds, some with known names, others unrecognizable, for which English titles are adopted. See *Thesmoph.* v. 331. The arguments used by Kock to prove that the interjected remarks belong to the Chorus, not to Peithetaerus, are hardly strong enough to remove the improbability that the poet would, in any part except the Parabasis, ascribe to the Birds so intimate a knowledge of Athenian manners and customs as these remarks contain.

Peithetaerus.

Hail, Sunium-worshipp'd Hawk; hail, royal Stork.

Priest.

and to the Pythian and Delian Swan; and to Lato,
Mother-quail, and Artemis the Goldfinch—   924

Peithetaerus.

Now no more Kolaenis, she Goldfinch Artemis will be.

Priest.

and to the Redstart Sabazian, and to the Sparrow,
mighty Mother of gods and men—

Peithetaerus.

O lady Kybele, be good to us, O Sparrow, Mother of
Kleokritus.

---

922 (869). Kock justly observes that, before this verse, some words of the liturgy must have been lost, in which Poseidon (Neptune) was addressed, as (the hawk) adored at Sunium, and as sea-king. This verse evidently refers to Poseidon, one of whose titles was 'Souniaratos, adored at Sunium,' the southern promontory of Attika, where he had a temple: another was 'Pelagikos, god of the sea.' The former of these is here made 'Sounierakos, Sunian hawk,' the latter 'Pelargikos (anax), stork-king.'

925 (871). "Kolaenis," an ancient and mysterious title of Artemis.

928 (875). "Sparrow." Kock is probably right in saying that Kybele is jocularly called 'sparrow' rather than 'ostrich.' The joke is heightened by contrast with her title 'Great Mother.'

928 (877). "Kleokritus." This person is mentioned again in *The Frogs*, v. 1437, but not so as to determine whether he was very large (as the Scholiast there represents) or the reverse; we must suppose the latter if Kybele is called 'sparrow,' not 'ostrich.'

Priest.
and to Olympian birds and lady-birds all, with united
prayer we call, that to Cloudcuckooburgesses they grant
health and wealth and all they want, themselves and
their alliance, especially the Chians— 932

Peithetaerus.
That's delicious, I declare: Chians tack'd on everywhere!

Priest.
and to each hero-bird and hero's son, and to pelican
and porphyrion; and to heathcock and blackcock, and
peacock; and to gannet, and heron, and grosbeak, and
shrike, and screechowl; and to blackcap, and titmouse,
and earlytrumpetfowl—

Peithetaerus.
A plague on all this nonsense! cease to bawl.
Ho, ho! what victim's this to which you call 940
Ospreys and vultures, dolt? a single kite,
D'ye see, could swoop and carry off this mite.
Clear out from us, and take your wreaths away:
I'll make this sacrifice myself to day.
[*Exit Priest.*

Chorus.
So now again a second strain   *Antistrophe.*
I must raise and not refrain: 946

---

932 (879). "The Chians." The Chians, before the Sicilian defeat,
were the most faithful allies of Athens, and received the honour
of being specially mentioned in Athenian liturgies.

939—44 (889—894). Peithetaerus, tired by the recital of so
many names, and finding the victim to be a small lean goat, dis-
misses the priest.

While they bear the sacred lotion,
I must set my songs in motion,
And to this our solemn rite
All the blessèd gods invite: 950
No, not all; one alone,
If indeed there's meat for one.
In the victim standing by
Only beard and horns I spy. 954

Peithetaerus.

Let us pray and sacrifice to the feather'd deities.

Enter Poet.

Poet.

Of Cloudcuckooborough's city
Celebrate the happy state,
O my Muse, in hymnèd ditty.

Peithetaerus.

What importation's this? say who you are.

---

955 (903), &c. Peithetaerus, preparing to sacrifice, is interrupted by a succession of applicants, who propose to settle themselves in the new city. First comes a poet, celebrating the city in lyric verse; then a soothsayer, with oracles: then Meton, the geometer, who offers his services as surveyor; next an inspector with a commission from Athens: finally a vender of plebiscites. The poet receives contemptuous alms; the others are dismissed with more or less severity. Then (as bloodshed on the stage was inadmissible) Peithetaerus removes the goat for sacrifice elsewhere, and leaves the Chorus to chant a second Parabasis.

956 (904), &c. The poet parodies (often, no doubt, using the original words) an ode addressed by Pindar to Hiero king of Syracuse, on occasion of the foundation of the city of Aetna.

Poet.
One who honey-voiced song produces,   960
A holy menial of the Muses:
Such is the title Homer uses.

Peithetaerus.
A slave are you, yet keep your flowing hair?

Poet.
No; but every one that song produces
Is a holy menial of the Muses;   965
Such is the title Homer uses.

Peithetaerus.
Your blouse too's holy; to your trade you owe it:
But what the mischief brings you here, Sir poet?

Poet.
Fine odes I've made and many, to renown
In song Cloudcuckooborough, your new town,   970
Some Cyclian, others Parthenean,
Others in style Simonidean.

---

961 (909). "Holy menial:" lit. *'diligent servant.'* The word 'holy' is substituted in the translation, to keep up the joke in v. 967 (915), which the Greek word for 'diligent' favours. In Homer's extant poems 'diligent servant' often occurs, but not with the case 'of the Muses' added.

963 (911). "Hair." Slaves had their hair clipt. The poet had called himself 'a menial of the Muses.'

971 (918). "Cyclian:" i.e. dithyrambic.

972 (919). "Parthenean:" i.e. to be sung by a chorus of virgins. "Simonidean:" Simonides of Keos had written much lyric and elegiac poetry. He died B.C. 469.

Peithetaerus.
When did you set about this song-inditing?

Poet.
Long on this city, long have I been writing.

Peithetaerus.
What? haven't I held its name-feast now, you gaby,
And called it for the first time, like a baby? 976

Poet.
By the Muses tidings swift are carried;
Swifter than the glancing force
Of the lightning-footed horse
Came the news, and never tarried. 980
But, O sacred-titled lord,
Founder and sire of Aetna's state,
What thy bounty can afford,
Be it little, be it great,
With a generous soul incline 985
To bestow on mine from thine.

Peithetaerus.
This plaguy wretch will worry us, I see,
If we don't shut his mouth up with a fee.
You've got a jerkin there, come, strip, bestow it
Upon my very learned friend the poet. 990
[*To one of the slaves.*

---

973 (920). When did you, &c. (when did you make these? from what *distance of* time?)

977—9 (924—5). By the Muses...tarried (but a swift one is the rumour of the Muses, such as the *glancing* speed of horses).

988 (932). If we, &c. (if we shall not escape by giving him something).

989 (933). A jerkin (a jerkin and a tunic).

There, poet, take this jerkin for your meed;
Your shivering plainly shews it what you need.

Poet.
Glad the friendly Muse receiveth
What the gracious donor giveth;
Yet expand your mental ear,   995
And a verse of Pindar hear.

Peithetaerus.
We shan't get quit of him just yet, 'tis clear.

Poet.
In the nomad Skythian's plain
Wanders ever, cold and lonely,
Straton with a jerkin only;   1000
Jerkin only, 'tis notorious,
Without tunic is inglorious.
Duly comprehend the strain.

Peithetaerus.
You want the tunic: that I comprehend.
Come, strip: one must assist a poet friend,   1005
[*To the slave.*
There, take it and be off.

Poet.
         I go: yet stay,
The city must receive this parting lay.
Seated on thy golden throne,

---

992 (935). Your shivering, &c. (you certainly seem to me to shiver).
993—996 (937—40). Glad—hear (this gift the friendly Muse receives not unwilling; but thou with thy heart learn a verse of Pindar).
998—1000 (941—3). In the, &c. (among the nomad Skythians wanders Straton who hath not acquired a woven wind-tossed vestment).

Muse, prepare a noble ditty
For the quivering, shivering city.   1010
To the snow-propelling zone,
The many-path'd, I hied awa',
      Tralalala!

Peithetaerus.

But now the tunic's on your back, my friend,
Of quivering and of shivering there's an end.   1015
                              [*Exit Poet.*
I can't conceive how to this rascal went
Such early notice of our settlement.
Boy, carry round again the laver. So.
Silence!

Enter a Soothsayer.

Soothsayer.
    Commence not on the goat.

Peithetaerus.
                    Hilloa!
What's here?

Soothsayer.
  A soothsayer.

Peithetaerus.
                    Bad luck be thine!   1020

Soothsayer.
Cast not contempt, great Sir, on things divine:
Here is an oracle of Bakis: see:
It fits Cloudcuckooborough perfectly.

    1022 (962). "Bakis." An ancient soothsayer of Bœotia. See Holden's *Onomastikon*.

Peithetaerus.
Then, ere I coloniz'd this city, why
Came you not here, and sang your prophecy?   1025

Soothsayer.
The spirit hindered then.

Peithetaerus.
                     Well, well! rehearse:
There's no great harm in listening to your verse.

Soothsayer.
'But when the wolves and hoary crows unite
To build 'twixt Sikyon and great Korinth's height'—

Peithetaerus.
And with Korinthians what concern have I?   1030

1027 (966). "Verse." Oracles were composed in the heroic rhythm of Homer. They usually commence with 'but,' being supposed to be extracts from a continuous collection of the Laws of Fate, like the Sibylline Books at Rome. Many such collections were preserved, private as well as public, bearing the names of ancient soothsayers such as Bakis. And those who retailed and recited these pretended oracles took the title of soothsayers like the personage here introduced by Aristophanes. See *The Peace*, v. 1052.

1028 (967). "Wolves and crows:" i.e. men and birds; beings of widely different natures.

1029 (968). "Sikyon and great Korinth's height." The land 'between Korinth and Sikyon' is mentioned in an ancient oracle cited by Athenaeus and Eustathius, as fertile (according to the latter author). Orneae (Birdtown, see v. 409) was on the confines of Sikyonia, but not on the road between Korinth and Sikyon.

1030 (969). The "Korinthians" were bitter enemies of the Athenians, and excited the allies to declare war against them, B.C. 431. See Thuk. I.

Soothsayer.

This hint of Bakis indicates the sky.
'Bid first in honour of Pandora bleed
A white-fleec'd ram: and then, as fitting meed
For the first prophet who my songs shall bear,
A goodly coat and sandals new prepare.'   1035

Peithetaerus.

They're in it too, the sandals?

Soothsayer.

      Take the book.
And, furthermore, the prophecy commands
'To give a cup, and fill with tripe his hands.'

Peithetaerus.

And giving tripe is in it?

Soothsayer.

      Take the book.
'And if thou doest my bidding, reverend Childe,   1040
An eagle in the clouds shalt thou be styled:
But if thou giv'st not, never shalt thou prove
Throstle or woodpecker or turtledove.'

Peithetaerus.

And is all this included?

Soothsayer.

      Take the book.

1032 (971). "Pandora;" i.e. 'the all-giving goddess,' naturally invoked by the begging soothsayer.

Peithetaerus.

Your oracle is not like this of mine, 1045
Which I got copied from Apollo's shrine.
'But when some swindler, uninvited there,
Disturbs the sacrifice, and tripe would share,
Let well-belabour'd ribs be all his fare.'

Soothsayer.

I think you're talking nonsense.

Peithetaerus.

Take the book. 1050
'Nor spare e'en eagle in the clouds, though he
Or Lampon or great Diopeithes be.'
Out, vermin, out! [*Beats him.*

Soothsayer.

Alack and welladay!

Peithetaerus.

Get out, and soothsay somewhere else: away!
[*Exit Soothsayer.*

Enter METON.

Meton.

I'm come to join you.

1045 (981). Peithetaerus 'trumps' the pretended oracle of Bakis with an oracle of Apollo, the god of prophecy; and expels the soothsayer ignominiously.

1052 (988). "Lampon:" see v. 548 (521). "Diopeithes;" another notorious soothsayer of the time, who pretended to divine inspiration. See Holden's *Onom.*: also *The Knights*, v. 1085; Xen. *Hell.* III. 3. He seems to have lived to a great age.

1055 (992). "Meton:" the famous mathematician and geometer, who invented a new calendar (the cycle of Meton). He

Peithetaerus.
            Here's another pest.   1055
What are you come for? what's the ideal thought,
What the design, the boot, of this your journey?

                Meton.
I want to measure geometrically
Your atmosphere, and map it out in acres.

                Peithetaerus.
And, in heaven's name, who are you?

                Meton.
                        Meton I,   1060
To Hellas and Kolonus known.

                Peithetaerus.
                        And these,
What are they?
                Meton.
            Rules for measuring the atmosphere.
For instance, all the atmosphere in shape
Is like a stove, as near as can be: so
When I my lineal fix, and from above   1065
Insert a pair of flexile compasses—
You comprehend?
                Peithetaerus.
            I do not comprehend.

---

resided in the Kolonus Agoraeus, near the Stoa Poekile: and is said to have erected there an astronomical instrument. See Holden's *Onom.*, which cites Leake's *Topography of Athens*, p. 219.

Meton.

A straight rule I apply to measure with,
That so your circle may become quadrangular,
With market-place i' the middle, whither lead   1070
Straight roads converging to the very centre:
And thus, as from a star, being circular,
Straight rays may flash their light in all directions.

Peithetaerus.

The man's a second Thales. Meton—

Meton.
      Well?   1074

Peithetaerus.

I'm your good friend, believe me; take my counsel,
And move, without disturbance, out o' the way.

Meton.

What danger is there?

Peithetaerus.
    As in Lakedaemon,
Aliens are banish'd, feelings are excited,
And many stripes are stirring through the city.

Meton.

Is discord raging here?

Peithetaerus.
    No, not at all.   1080

1078 (1013). "Aliens are banish'd." The allusion is to the laws of Lakedaemon, by which foreigners were not allowed to reside there. In the latter part of this verse the conjecture of Kock is adopted: "feelings are excited."

Meton.
What is the matter then?

Peithetaerus.
In perfect concord
We are resolved to kick out every humbug.

Meton.
I must be gone then.

Peithetaerus.
Yes: I'm not quite sure
You've time: here are the stripes, impending now.
[*Beats him.*

Meton.
Me miserable!

Peithetaerus.
Did'nt I give you warning?   1085
Remeasure yourself and be off elsewhere.
[*Exit Meton.*

Enter an Inspector.

Inspector.
Where are the consuls?

Peithetaerus.
Who's this dainty don?

1087 (1021). The person who now enters professes to be an inspector elected at Athens by lottery of beans to visit Cloudcuckoo-borough in that character. Such inspectors were sent out to subject states with a certain authority analogous to that of modern 'governors.' Those employed by the Lakedaemonians were called 'harmostai.' "The consuls," Gr. 'proxenoi.' This office corresponded very nearly to that of those who are now called 'consuls,' that is, residents in a foreign city, whose duty it is to provide there

Inspector.
I'm an inspector by the bean elected
To this Cloudcuckooborough.
Peithetaerus.
An inspector?
Who sent you here?
Inspector.
A certain trumpery warrant   1090
Of Teleas.
Peithetaerus.
Will you take your salary then,
Not bore us, but be gone?
Inspector.
With all my heart.
I wish'd to stay at home and sit in parliament:
Some foreign business I have done with Pharnakes.
Peithetaerus.
Take it and go then. That's your salary.   1095
[*Beats him.*

---

for the interests and requirements of the state which employs them. Anciently they were citizens of the place itself in which they were employed: in modern times very rarely so.

"Dainty don;" lit. '*Sardanapalus*,' the luxurious king of Assyria. The presumptuous affectation of the inspector's dress and manner procures for him this title.

1091 (1025). "Teleas:" see v. 180 (168).

1093 (1027). "To sit in parliament:" lit. '*to attend the Ekklesia*' or Assembly of all Athenian citizens, in which great public affairs were discussed and determined.

1094 (1028). "Pharnakes;" the Persian satrap of Daskylitis in Asia. At this time the support of the Persian power began to be zealously sought by both the contending Hellenic parties.

Inspector.

What's this?

Peithetaerus.

A sitting of the house on Pharnakes.

Inspector.

I call you all to witness I am beaten,
I, an inspector.

Peithetaerus.

Shoo! shoo! wo'nt you scud,
And take your brace of ballot-boxes with you?

[*Exit Inspector.*

Now is not this a scandal? To our city   1100
Already they are sending out inspectors
Before our sacrifices are performed.

Enter a Plebiscite-vender.

Plebiscite-vender.

'If any Cloudcuckooburgess wrong an Athenian—'

Peithetaerus.

What plague again is here? what manuscript?

1099 (1032). The inspector had brought with him two ballot-urns, for the purpose of holding elections and official lotteries in the new city.

1103 (1035). The last intruder is a "vender of plebiscites," Gr. 'of psephisms.' A psephism was a decree of the Assembly, for which, though not having all legal formality, the force of law was claimed. Aristotle (*Pol.* IV. 4) and Cicero (*Rep.* I. 27) notice this as an extreme form of democracy, carried out by demagogues. As such decrees became numerous, copies of them were made and sold for use at home and abroad. Such is the trade of the personage who now appears. He calls his psephisms 'new laws.'

[EPEISODION II.]   *THE BIRDS.*

Plebiscite-vender.

Vender of plebiscites am I; new laws 1105
I'm come amongst you here to sell.

Peithetaerus.

Sell what?

Plebiscite-vender.

'For Cloudcuckooburgesses we decree that all the measures and weights shall be the same as those of Poland.' 1109

Peithetaerus.

Yours soon shall be the same as those of Woland.

[*Beats him.*

Plebiscite-vender.

Sir, what do you mean?

Peithetaerus.

Go, take away your laws.
I'll sharpen them for you to-day, those laws.

[*Exit Plebiscite-vender.*

1108 (1041). "As those of Poland:" lit. '*as those of the Olophyxians.*' Olophyxus was a colony on the Thracian coast near Mount Athos.

1110 (1042). "As those of Woland:" lit. '*as those of the Ototyxians.*' The *jeu de mots* here is imitated by using the name *Poland* for 'Olophyxians,' and *Woland* for 'Ototyxians,' which latter is a mere comically invented word, having no local existence. As Olophyxus resembles a Greek verb meaning *to bewail*, so Ototyxus is designed to recall another verb, which means *to cry* or *howl.*

Inspector [*from the side*].

I summon Peithetaerus for assault, to appear at the April sessions without default.

Peithetaerus.

Oh, really, you're amongst us, are you, still?   1115

Plebiscite-vender [*from the side*].

'If any shall drive out the magistrates, and not receive them, as the column states—'

Peithetaerus.

O cruel fate! and you're amongst us still?

Inspector [*from the side*].

I'll ruin you in damages, I will.
I'll lay them at ten thousand drachmas, Sir.   1120

Peithetaerus.

I'll scatter to the winds your ballot-boxes.

Plebiscite-vender [*from the side*].

Your insult to the column once at even,
Remember that.

Peithetaerus.

    Faugh, faugh! let some one seize him.
Oh, you won't tarry, won't you?—From this place
Let us as soon as possible go in   1125
And sacrifice unto the gods the goat.

[*Exeunt all but Chorus.*

1117 (1050). "The column". Columns were erected in public places, on which were engraven the terms of treaties between contracting states.

Chorus.
(Ode).

Through the coming ages now	*Strophe.*
With the sacrifice and vow	
Mortals shall to me be praying,	
Me the allseeing and allswaying,	1130
Me whose active sight extends	
To the earth's extremest ends.	
I preserve the blooming fruit,	
Slaying every noxious brute:	
Such as with rapacious jaw	1135
Under ground the rootlets gnaw;	
Such as, lurking in the boughs,	
On the budding fruitage browze:	
I destroy the loathsome swarm	
That with foul pollution harm	1140
All the garden's fragrant charm:	
Biting creatures, creatures crawling,	
Bleed beneath my pinions sprawling.	

(Epirrhema).

Specially, however, it is notified to-day,	
Melian Diagoras if any of you slay,	1145

1127 (1058). The second Parabasis here begins. It has no kommation, and no anapaestic address or parabasis in the narrower sense. The ode asserts the divine nature and influence now belonging to the Birds. The epirrhema is a ludicrous 'hue and cry' after various offenders against their dignity. The antode is an exquisite poetic description of the joys of birdlife. The antepirrhema pretends to win the favour of the judges by promises and threats of a highly comic character.

1145 (1073). "Melian Diagoras." Diagoras of Melos had been (about ten years before the date of this play) obliged to

Your reward's a talent; and a talent for the head
Shall be paid of any of the tyrants that are dead.
Also we do thus declare our high and mighty will :—
Sparrower Philokrates if any of you kill,
You will get a talent; if alive he's taken, four; 1150
For he strings and sells the finches at a groat a score,
Blows the fieldfares out and shews 'em with insulting grin,
To the nozzles of the blackbirds sticks the feathers in ;
Pigeons that he catches in his cages all are set, 1154
And must be decoy-birds for him, fastened in a net.
Thus do we proclaim. And if by any of you men
Birds are kept in aviaries, let them loose again.
Our police shall seize you, if this warning you defy,
And in penal servitude decoying men you'll lie.

(*Antode*).
Happy are the feathered folk, 1160
Who in winter wear no cloak ;

1151 (1079). At a groat a score (at the rate of seven for an obol).

---

fly from Athens to escape a capital charge of impiety and atheism. A price was set on him, but the people of Pellene, where he found refuge, would not give him up. As he is here ludicrously coupled with the dead tyrants, he was probably no longer alive, and Grote (II. lviii.) must be considered wrong in assigning the prosecution against him to the year B.C. 415. In *The Clouds*, v. 830, Sokrates is called 'the Melian,' that is 'the atheist,' in allusion to this Diagoras. See also *The Frogs*, v. 320.

As in this passage the poet unquestionably glances at the measures taken against the suspected Hermokopidae, it throws important light on his political feeling at the time when this play was written. See Introduction.

1149 (1077). "Philokrates." See v. 14.

And the summer does not burn us
With its hot far-flashing furnace:
But in flowery meads I dwell,
Lingering oft in leafy dell, 1165
When the inspired cicala's gladness,
Swelling into sunny madness,
Filleth all the fervid noon
With its shrill and ceaseless tune.
But throughout the wintry day 1170
In some hollow cave I stay
With the mountain nymphs at play.
Myrtle-berries, spring-bedew'd,
White and tender, are my food,
And a thousand delicacies 1175
From the gardens of the Graces.

(*Antepirrhema*).

On the victory I wish a word or two to say,
How the judges all will gain by voting for our play,
Getting better gifts than those of Paris far away.

1179 (1104). "Paris:" Gr. 'Alexander,' (son of Priam,) called by both these names. When he was chosen to adjudge the golden apple, as prize of beauty, to one of the three competing goddesses (Hera, Pallas, Aphrodite), he was promised various gifts by each on condition of deciding in favour of the promiser. So the Birds jocularly promise the judges various good things if they vote the first prize to this Comedy. These are (1) Laureotic *owls*, that is, plenty of money; coins, made from the silver of the mines of Laurium, or Laureium, in Attika, bearing the image of an owl: (2) pinnacles to the roofs of their houses shaped in the so-called *eagle* style (aëtomata): (3) assistance from a *hawk* in the work of peculation: (4) the loan of *crows* to eat good dinners with. On the other hand, if the votes are refused, they threaten to spoil the best clothes of the recalci-

First—for more than anything each judge has this at
    heart— 1180
Never shall the Laureotic owls from you depart,
But shall in your houses dwell, and in your purses too
Nestle close, and hatch a brood of little coins for
    you.
Furthermore we'll let you live in temples like the gods,
Eagle-fashion'd pinnacles adorning your abodes. 1185
If, in some poor office plac'd, to pilfering you incline,
We will lend a small sharp hawk to favour your
    design;
Craws too we will send you when you're going out to
    dine.
But, if you reject us, then let each a little shed
Forge, like lunes o'er statues, as a shelter for his head;
Lest, without it when you walk in clean and white
    attire, 1191
All the birds their vengeance take by covering you
    with mire.

Enter PEITHETAERUS.

Peithetaerus.

Our sacrifices, Birds, are favourable:
But from the works no messenger arrives

---

trant judges. These inducements were not irresistible, as Aristophanes obtained only the second prize in this competition.

    1190 (1114). "Lunes:" Gr. 'meniskoi,' semicircular tin sheds erected over statues in the open air, to protect them from the weather and from defilement.

    1193—1248 (1118—67). Peithetaerus, having sacrificed the goat with favourable omens, returns, expecting a report from the builders.

To tell us how the business there goes on. 1195
Nay, here comes one at last, and running too
And panting in the true Alphean style.

Enter First Messenger.

First Messenger.
Where, where is—where, where, where is—where is he,
The archon Peithetaerus?

Peithetaerus.
He is here.

First Messenger.
Your wall is finish'd.

Peithetaerus.
Thanks for your good tidings.

First Messenger.
A very noble and magnificent structure. 1201
So vast the breadth is, that upon the top
Proxenides of Bragham and Theogenes

A messenger arrives, and gives a comic narrative of the manner in which the works have been executed by the birds, who have put forth all that strength of which they boasted in v. 668 (637).

1197 (1121). "Panting in the true Alphean style:" lit. *'breathing Alpheus:'* i.e. 'panting like a tired foot-racer at Olympia,' where the river Alpheus skirted the raceground.

1203 (1126). "Theogenes" has been before cited as a poor braggart who pretended to be richer than he was. See v. 867 (822): he appears again v. 1376 (1295). "Proxenides" is one of the same stamp, a 'kapnos' or 'man of smoke.' Aristophanes invents for him a new deme, 'Kompasai,' i.e. 'Bragham.'

Could drive two passing chariots clear, with steeds
Big as the wooden one of old.

Peithetaerus.

      Great Herakles! 1205

First Messenger.

The height (I measured it myself) is just
A hundred fathoms.

Peithetaerus.

    What a height, Poseidon!
Who built it up to such enormous size?

First Messenger.

Birds and none else: no bricklayer of Aegypt,
No stonehewer was there, no carpenter: 1210
With their own hands they did it, to my marvel.
There came from Libya thirty thousand cranes,
All having swallowed down foundation stones,
Which with their beaks the rails still aptly shaped:
Another party of ten thousand storks   1215
Were brickmakers: and water from below
The plovers and the other wading birds
Were raising up into the higher air.

  1205 (1128). "Wooden one:" i.e. the wooden horse by which Troy was taken. See Verg. *Aen.* II.

  1213 (1137). "Foundation stones." The Greeks had a false notion that cranes carried stones as ballast to steady their flight.

  1214 (1138). "The rails." The true English title of the bird here ('krex') is uncertain, but it corresponds in some respects to 'the rail' (rallus).

Peithetaerus.
And who conveyed the mortar for them?
First Messenger.
Herons,
In hods.
Peithetaerus.
And how did they get in the mortar?   1220
First Messenger.
That was the cleverest device of all, Sir.
The geese with their web-feet, as though with spades,
Dipp'd down, and laid it neatly on the hods.
Peithetaerus.
What feat indeed may not be wrought by feet?
First Messenger.
Ay, and the ducks, by Jove, all tightly girt,   1225
Kept carrying bricks, and *other birds* were flying
With trowel on their heads, *to lay the bricks*...
And then, like children *sucking lollipops,*
The swallows *minced* the mortar in their mouths.
Peithetaerus.
Why should one hire paid labourers any more?   1230

1224 (1147). "Feet:" jocularly substituted by Aristophanes for 'hands,' which is the original word in the proverb cited.

1228—29 (1149—51). There is a loss here of one and a half, or two and a half Greek lines, so that we cannot say what birds they were that took the trowels and laid the bricks. The words in italics are inserted to supply the probable sense. The preparation of the mud by the swallows is evidently likened to the sucking of sweetmeats by children, though verb and object are lost.

Well now, what next? who were the birds that wrought
The woodwork of the fort?

First Messenger.
     Skill'd carpenters,
The yellow-hammers: with their hammering beaks
They finish'd off the gates: the noise they made
In hammering was exactly like a shipyard.   1235
The fortress has its portals firmly fitted,
Supplied with bolts and bars, and guarded round:
The beats are paced: the bell is borne: the watch
At every point established, and the beacons
Set on the towers.—But I must run away   1240
And clean myself. Look you, Sir, to the rest.
       [*Exit First Messenger.*

Chorus.
Sir, what's the matter with you? do you marvel
The fortress has been finish'd with such speed?

Peithetaerus.
Ay, by the gods: a wondrous work it is:

  1233 (1155). "Yellow-hammers." The birds here named by Aristophanes are 'pelicans,' chosen merely for the play of sound between that bird's name and the verb 'pelekân,' 'to hew in shape.' The translation substitutes a different bird for a similar purpose.

  1238 (1160). "The bell." This was borne by the sentinel in his rounds to shew that he was not asleep. See v. 891 (842).

  1242 (1164). Peithetaerus remains for a while wrapt in meditation, till addressed by the Chorus. This device, with their short dialogue (says Dindorf), gives the actor (tritagonist) who plays the part of Messenger time to alter his dress, and appear again as one of the guards.

  1245 (1167). It is hardly necessary to call attention to the exquisite humour of this verse.

In very truth it looks to me like fiction.   1245
But wait a moment: here's a messenger,
One of the guards from thence, who's running to us
With face as martial as a pyrrhich-dance.

Second Messenger.

What ho! what ho! what ho! what ho! what ho!

Peithetaerus.

Well, what's the matter?

Second Messenger.

Very shameful treatment!   1250
One of those gods from Zeus's place just now
Flew through our gates into the atmosphere,
All unobserved of our day-scouts, the jays.

Peithetaerus.

O shameful deed and unendurable!
Which of the gods?

Second Messenger.

We know not. Wings it had,   1255
We know.

Peithetaerus.

Your course then, surely, was to launch
Some yeomanry upon its track.

1248 (1169). Lit. '*looking a pyrrhich-dance.*' This famous war-dance, imitating martial gestures, is said to take its name from the inventor.

1249 (1170). The guard enters to announce the appearance and pursuit of Iris the rainbow-goddess.

1257 (1177). "Yeomanry:" Gr. 'peripoloi.' These were young men after the age of eighteen, a sort of 'landwehr' force, enlisted to watch and protect the Attic frontiers.

Second Messenger.
                We did:
Our mounted archers, thirty thousand hawks,
We sent, all riding with their claws acrook,
Falcon and buzzard, vulture, nightjar, eagle: 1260
Hark! with the rush and whirring of their wings
All ether shudders, as they seek the god.
Far off it cannot be: indeed I think
'Tis here already.
                Peithetaerus.
                Must we not get slings   1264
And bows and arrows? Henchmen all, look out:
Shoot, smite: supply me, some one, with a sling.
                [*Exit Peithetaerus with Second Messenger.*
                Chorus.
War is rising, war surprising,   *Strophe.*
War between the gods and me;
So let every watchbird see
That this, the child of Erebus,   1270

1267 (1189), &c. Peithetaerus here quits the stage to assist in the pursuit of Iris. Meanwhile the Chorus chants a first Chorikon (Strophe), inspiriting the Bird-troops to their 'sacred war': after which Iris appears flying, by means of machinery, across the scene. Peithetaerus rushes in, pursuing her; and by a concealed ledge she is able to pause and sustain the dialogue with him, at the close of which the machine wafts her away again. That dialogue itself sparkles with admirable humour; and the parody of tragic style scattered through it must have greatly amused an Athenian audience, whose ears and minds were, by the annual Dionysiac contests, thoroughly trained to perceive and appreciate the tone of a Sophokles or Euripides. On the treatment which the gods receive here and afterwards see the Introduction.

[EPEISODION III.] *THE BIRDS.* 111

Our cloud-encircled atmosphere,
Be guarded strictly, far and near,
Lest any god should pass unseen of us.
Look out, look out, each careful scout, around, about.
Some daemon's whirling through the lofty sky: 1275
E'en now the wingèd sound approaches nigh.

      IRIS *appears flying across the scene.*
      Peithetaerus re-entering.
Ho, madam, whither, whither, whither flying?
Stay quiet there; be still; restrain your course.
Who and what are you? Whence arrived? declare.

      Iris.
I'm from the realm of the Olympian gods.   1280

      Peithetaerus.
And what are we to call you? bark or bonnet?

      Iris.
Swift Iris.

      Peithetaerus.
   Paralus or Salaminia?

   1281 (1203). "Bark or bonnet." The grotesque apparel of Iris suggests this strange question. Wearing a huge loose robe floating behind her person she recalls the image of a ship in full sail. Having on her head a 'kunê' or Arcadian bonnet-hat with wide brims for protection from the sun (see Soph. *Oed. C.* v. 314) and perhaps painted with rainbow colours, Peithetaerus gives her that title as an alternative.
   1282 (1204). "Swift Iris." Peithetaerus, pretending to infer from this answer that she is a vessel, humorously asks if she is one or other of the Athenian state galleys, Paralus or Salaminia. See v. 155 (147).

Iris.

What means this?

Peithetaerus.

Won't some buzzard soar and seize her?

Iris.

Seize me? What mischief's here?

Peithetaerus.

We'll make you smart.

Iris.

All this is monstrous folly.

Peithetaerus.

By what gate   1285
Came you within the fort, you shameless jade?

Iris.

I have no notion, really, by what gate.

Peithetaerus.

You hear how she prevaricates. Did you
Appear before the jay-chiefs? Won't you answer?
Have you a passport from the storks?

Iris.

What stuff's this? 1290

Peithetaerus.

You've got none?

Iris.

Are you sane?

Peithetaerus.
                          Did no bird-captain
Attend and set a label on your person?

Iris.
None set a label on my person, wretch.

Peithetaerus.
And would you with such silent secrecy
Fly through a foreign city and through Chaos?   1295

Iris.
And by what other road are gods to fly?

Peithetaerus.
I have no notion, really; not by this.
You're guilty, let me tell you: long ere now
You ought to have been seized and put to death,
No Iris in the world with greater justice,   1300
If you'd got your deserts.

Iris.
           But I'm immortal.

Peithetaerus.
You should have died in spite of that. Our case
Will be a cruel one, methinks, if, whilst
We're ruling all the rest, you gods alone
Take every kind of license, not yet knowing   1305
That you in your turn must obey your betters.
But tell me, whither do you steer your wings?

Iris.
What, I? I'm flying on my father's errand,
To bid men offer to the Olympian gods,

8

And on their bullock-sacrificing hearths   1310
To slaughter sheep, and fill the streets with savour.

Peithetaerus.
What's this you're saying? Offer to what gods?

Iris.
What gods? to us, the gods that are in heaven.

Peithetaerus.
Are you then gods?

Iris.
What other gods exist?

Peithetaerus.
Birds unto men are gods: to them must men   1315
Now sacrifice, and not, by Jove, to Jove.

Iris.
O fool, fool! anger not the hearts of gods,
But fear, lest Justice with the spade of Zeus
Thy race in utter ruin overthrow,
The torch thy body and thy circling domes   1320
Reduce to cinders with Likymnian bolts.

Peithetaerus.
Hark'ee, my lady! cease your shrewish rant;
Be still; with words like these, I wish to know,

1321 (1242). "Likymnian bolts." Euripides wrote a tragedy called Likymnius; and this passage is perhaps parodied from that drama: but in what sense (if sense here is to be looked for) bolts are called 'Likymnian,' we have no means of knowing. Perhaps Likymnius in the play is killed by lightning.

Lydian or Phrygian do you think to scare?
If Zeus disturb us longer—mark me well—   1325
His palace and Amphion's domes will I
Reduce to cinders with fire-carrying eagles:
And, warring on him, I'll despatch to heaven
Magogian birds, in pardskin uniforms,
Above six hundred by the tale; and once   1330
He found a single Magog troublesome.
And, mistress Iris, if you shew your airs,
You'll not get off scot-free. Return again
To give us further trouble, and you'll find
My harem has a vacant place for you.   1335

Iris.

Perdition seize you, wretch, with your vile language.

Peithetaerus.

Shoo! shoo! be off, and suddenly: quick march!

Iris.

My sire will quell your insolence, I swear.

1324 (1244). "Lydian or Phrygian." This is taken from the *Alkestis* of Euripides, v. 675, where Pheres says in answer to the reproaches of his son Admetus:

'Is it some Lydian or Phrygian slave
Bought with thy money thou dost thus upbraid?'

1326 (1246). "Amphion's domes:" a parody from the Niobe of Aeschylus.

1329 (1249). "Magogian birds:" Gr. 'porphyrions;' harmless seabirds, chosen by Aristophanes here, to suggest the giant whom Horace calls 'minaci Porphyrion statu.' See v. 584 (553).

1332 (1253). The latter part of this speech is substituted, not translated.

8—2

Peithetaerus.

Dear, dear! how very sad! come, fly away,
Fly, and reduce to cinders some small child.   1340
[*Exit Iris.*

Chorus.

We're excluding all intruding   *Antistrophe.*
Of the Jove-descended gods;
Through our fortified abodes
Never may they travel more.
Nor by this road to gods again   1345
Shall savour rise of victims slain
On any mortal's sacrificial floor.

* * * * * *

Peithetaerus.

Too bad! that herald who was sent to mortals,
It seems as if he never would return.

Enter Herald.

Herald.

O Peithetaerus, O thou blest, thou wisest,   1350
O thou thrice blest and noblest, O thou smoothest,
Call silence, O call silence.

Peithetaerus.
What's your news?

1347 (1266). Comparison with the Strophic passage 1274—6 (1196—8) seems to shew that three lines are here lost.

1350 (1267), &c. The herald compliments Peithetaerus, gives him an account of the enthusiasm created among men by the foundation of his new city, and says that large crowds are coming to obtain wings.

Herald.
All people crown you with this golden crown
For your sagacious tact, and honour you.
Peithetaerus.
Thanks! Why am I thus honoured of the people?
Herald.
O founder of a most illustrious   1356
Etherial city, are you not aware
What honour you have won in men's esteem,
How many are enamoured of this land?
Until this city was establish'd by you,   1360
All men had been Lakonomaniacs;
They wore long hair, they fasted, they went dirty
Like Sokrates, they carried skytal-staves:

1353 (1274). "Golden crown." Such a gift was unusual at this date. After the battle of Salamis, olive crowns were voted to Eurybiades and Themistokles as rewards of valour. But we read in Thuk. IV. 121 that the people of Skione presented Brasidas with a golden crown. And this became usual at a later date, as witness the golden crown voted by the Athenians to Demosthenes the orator on the motion of Ktesiphon.

1361 (1281). "Lakonomaniacs." There was always a minority at Athens who inclined to Lakedaemonian habits and institutions. But in the Peloponnesian war they had become an eccentric and affected class, whose habits are here held up to ridicule.

1363 (1282). "Like Sokrates." The plain style of living adopted by Sokrates, caused him (as appears from *The Clouds*) to be classed with the affected Lakonists. The verb here used is one of comic coinage, implying *they had the Sokratic malady.*

"Carried skytal-staves." The 'skytale' was a staff invented at Sparta for the purpose of holding secret communication with generals and ambassadors. The 'skytalion' or small skytale was the Spartan walking-stick.

But now, converted, they've become birdmaniacs,
And in this new delight do everything   1365
That's done by birds, in mimicry of them.
First, when they wake at early morn, they'll fly
Together all to pasture, like ourselves,
And then they'll settle down upon the books,
And there continue feeding on decrees.   1370
So manifestly bird-mad are they that
To many men are given the names of birds.
One limping shopkeeper they call a partridge:
Menippus is a swallow, and Opuntius

1367—70 (1286—9). Kock says (perhaps justly) that the word 'nomos' here means 'pasture' only, and that the other meaning 'law' is not implied in it. The four lines are not free from obscurity; but we must probably consider that the play of words is contained in the verbs only, not in the objects. According to Kock, Aristophanes says that the Athenians, after an early breakfast (of bread soaked in wine), resorted to the bookshops to get the news of the day; and then (on business days) proceeded to the Pnyx to attend the assembly and consider decrees. So the birds are supposed to begin the day with pasturage, then to fly about and amuse themselves, and in the afternoon to take their principal meal.

1371—80 (1292—99). Of the persons named, Opuntius, Philokles and Theogenes have been already noticed. Probably Philokles is called a lark because he managed to get the prize in competition with the *Oedipus Rex* of Sophokles, and a proverb says that 'to unpoetic minds the lark is more melodious than the swan.' The vulpanser, or Aegyptian goose, which represents Theogenes, is described by Aelian as a cunning bird. The lame shopkeeper (or vintner) is unknown: Menippus equally so. Lykurgus is ridiculed as of Aegyptian blood; hence called 'ibis.' Chaerephon is the pallid companion of Sokrates; he appears in *The Clouds*, and

An eyeless raven; Philokles a lark; 1375
Theogenes vulpanser, and Lykurgus
Is term'd an ibis, Chaerephon a bat,
A magpie Syrakosius; Meidias
A quail they call, for he is like a quail
By a quail-smiter wounded in the head. 1380
And all from bird-delight are singing ballads,
In which is any mention of a swallow,
Of widgeon, goose, or woodpigeon, or wings,
Or e'en a slight suspicion of a feather.
Such tidings from that world. But one thing learn:
Ten thousand men or more will come to you 1386
From thence, desiring wings and crook-claw'd fashions:
So wings you must find somewhere for the comers.

Peithetaerus.

Faith, then, our business won't be standing still.
You there, set off with speed, and fill the hampers,
And every basket you can find, with wings. 1391

[*To a slave.*

Let Manes carry to me out of doors
Those wings: and I'll receive the visitors.

---

again in this play, v. 1655 (1564). Meidias kept quails, and, as he had a scar on the forehead, he is likened to a quail wounded in the game called 'quail-smiting,' which (as described by Pollux, IX. 109) consisted in filliping the quail's head or plucking out a feather, and, if the bird bore this without flinching, its master won; otherwise not. Syrakosius, a loquacious demagogue, had carried a law (for which the comic poet Phrynichus reviled him in *The Monotropus*, acted in competition with *The Birds*) forbidding comedies to be produced in which an individual was held up to continuous ridicule, as Kleon in *The Knights*, and Sokrates in *The Clouds*.

Chorus.

Ere long will human beings all *Strophe a.*
This place 'the many-peopled' call: 1395
If fortune smile, the coming age
Will see my city quite the rage.

Peithetaerus.

Why don't the wings come quicker out?

Chorus.

All that's beautiful and good *Strophe b.*
Will not every sojourner 1400
Find in ample measure here,
Wisdom, Love, ambrosial Graces,
And, happiest of happy faces,
The gentle-minded Quietude?

Peithetaerus.

This is idle work, my master; 1405
Stir your stumps a little faster. [*To Manes.*

Chorus. *Antistrophe a.*

A pannier here of wings! be quick:— [*To Manes.*
I hope you will not spare the stick:
Your blows, like us, Sir, on him shower,
No donkey in the world is slower. [*To Peithetaerus.*

Peithetaerus.

Yes, Manes is a fearful lout. 1411

1389—1419 (1308—1336). Peithetaerus and the Chorus, with slaves, busy themselves in the preparation of wings for mankind.

Chorus.

First, these wings within your reach,   *Antistrophe b.*
Musical, prophetical,
Maritime, assort them all:
Next, observe the coming faces,   1415
And, weighing well their various cases,
Assign the proper plumes to each.

Peithetaerus.

You'll catch it smartly, by the falcons, soon,
If still I find you such a lazy loon.   [*To Manes.*

Enter a would-be Parricide.

Parricide.

A high-flying eagle I would be   1420
To fly o'er the surge of the barren blue sea.

1412—14 (1332—3). The musical wings are for song-birds; the prophetical for birds of prey, which were considered oracular; the maritime for sea-birds.

1420 (1337), &c. Three specimens of the applicants for wings are introduced in the close of this Episode: (1) an unnatural son (called here a parricide) who, emulating the young cock, heretofore mentioned v. 799 (758), professes a wish to strangle his father, and get his property. Peithetaerus treats him more mildly than he seems to deserve, dissuades him from his evil design, and dressing him up as an 'orphanbird,' sends him to fight his country's battles in Thrace. (2) The dithyrambic poet Kinesias desires wings, which may enable him to soar into the clouds and there collect materials for his misty poetic preludes. Peithetaerus whips him out contemptuously. (3) An informer (sycophant) wants wings, in order to pursue his dishonest trade more safely and rapidly. He is packed off with indignant and severe flagellation. After which the Chorus, again left alone, chants a Stasimon, of which the Strophe

Peithetaerus.

Our herald's tale seems likely to be true:
Here comes a fellow singing about eagles.

Parricide.

Ho, ho! there's nothing half so sweet as flying:
I'm quite enamoured of the laws of birds.   1425
I've the bird-mania; yes, to fly I wish
And dwell with you; and I desire your laws.

Peithetaerus.

What laws d'ye mean? For birds have many laws.

Parricide.

Ail: chiefly that it's held a law of honour
In birds to strangle and to peck their fathers.   1430

Peithetaerus.

Ay, and in fact when a young cock stands up
And spurs his sire, we hold him very—manly.

Parricide.

Therefore I migrate hither, and desire
To choke my father, and possess his fortune.

---

describes the worthless Kleonymus, under the likeness of a marvellous tree; and the Antistrophe treats of the danger which Athenians incur on a dark night from the assaults of the cloak-robber Orestes.

1425 (1343). "The laws." As this term is four times repeated in a few lines, and again v. 1435, it seems almost certain that a *jeu de mots* is designed between 'nómos,' *law*, and 'nomós,' *pasture*.

Peithetaerus.

Yes, but we birds have got an ancient law   1435
Kept in the record-office of the storks,
That when the parent stork has reared his brood
And turn'd them out all capable of flying,
The storklings in their turn must feed their sire.

Parricide.

Much good then I had got from coming here,   1440
If I must e'en be made to feed my father.

Peithetaerus.

No, not at all: for since you came, poor wretch,
With friendly feelings to us, I'll contrive
To fit you, as an orphanbird, with wings.
But take this hint, young fellow, not a bad one,
Which I got in my boyhood: don't go back   1446
And beat your father: but receive this wing
In the one hand, and this spur in the other,
And wear this crest as 'twere a cock's: then go,
Serve both in garrison and in the field   1450
For soldier's pay: so let your father live;
And since your tastes are warlike, Thraceward fly,
And fight your fill there.

1444 (1362). "Orphanbird." The Greeks probably gave this name to some bird; but it is not identified.

1447—9 (1365—6). The "wing" here is represented by a shield, the "spur" by a spear, and the cock's "crest" by the crest of a helmet.

1452 (1369). "Thraceward." The Athenians were always more or less engaged in warfare with the turbulent colonies in Thrace and Makedonia. See Thuk. IV. v. They had not recovered Amphipolis (lost B.C. 422) at the date of this play.

Parricide.

    Ay, by Dionysus,
I deem your counsel good, and I'll obey
Your bidding.

    Peithetaerus.

  'Tis a wise resolve, by Jove.   1455
        [*Exit Parricide.*

   Enter KINESIAS.

    Kinesias.

Lightly with my wings I fly
To Olympian seats on high,
Fly to every varied strain
In the lyrical domain—

    Peithetaerus.

This creature's wanting a ship-load of feathers. 1460

    Kinesias.

With a mind's eye void of fear
Visiting the people here.

    Peithetaerus.

Kinesias the linden-man, all hail!
Why limpest hither lithely, lame of leg?

  1456 (1372). " Lightly, &c." This is parodied from Anakreon.
  1463 (1378). " Kinesias." This dithyrambic poet seems to have had an evil reputation both moral and literary. See Holden's *Onom.* In person he was slender, and on that account Peithetaerus calls him 'a man of lindenwood,' which is light and flexible.

Kinesias.

Let me be made a bird, I beg,   1465
A melodious nightingale.

Peithetaerus.

A truce to lyrics! Tell me what you want.

Kinesias.

I would be wing'd by you, and fly aloft,
And from the clouds obtain some preludes new,
Of air-elate and snow-propelling nature.   1470

Peithetaerus.

What? Can a man get preludes from the clouds?

Kinesias.

Yes, upon these alone our art depends.
All brilliant dithyrambs are airy things,
Dark, dimly-lighted, wing-rapt; only listen,
And you will quickly know.

Peithetaerus.
                    Indeed I won't.   1475

Kinesias.

Ah! but you shall, I vow by Herakles:
For I will traverse all your atmosphere,
And sing—Ye shades of flying ones, sky-floating
Neck-stretching birds—

1469 (1385). "Preludes." The first stave of a dithyrambic ode, accompanied by the 'kithara' or the lyre, was called a *prelude* (anabolé). Aristophanes here ridicules the frigid and far-fetched affectation of these compositions.

Peithetaerus.
I'll stop your boating.

Kinesias.
Wandering on the seaward track,   1480
Let me ride the windy rack—

Peithetaerus.
I'll take the wind out of your sails, I will.

Kinesias.
Now to the southern side careering,
Now to the north my body veering,
Ever cleaving, as I fly,   1485
Harbourless furrows of the sky—
Pretty and clever is your craft, old sire.
   [*Peithetaerus beats him with the wings.*

Peithetaerus.
There! don't you find it pleasant to be wing-rapp'd?

Kinesias.
Is this the way you treat the Cyclian teacher,
Me, whom the rival tribes each year contend for?   1490

   1479 (1395). "I'll stop your boating." This is expressed in Greek by a single cry 'ὄοπ' (=stop her) used by boatmen when the boat is to be brought to shore.

   1487 (1401). "Pretty, &c." Peithetaerus here exhibits a pair of wings, which Kinesias commends, but, instead of giving them to him, Peithetaerus uses them to whip the poet, and when he winces, asks if he does not like being 'wing-rapp'd,' parodying the word before used by Kinesias.

   1489 (1403). "Cyclian teacher." Dithyrambic poetry was called Cyclian, because it took its origin from songs sung by a

Peithetaerus.
Well, won't you stay with us awhile, and teach
For bursar Leotrophides a chorus
Of flying birds belonging to the Rail tribe?
Kinesias.
You're laughing at me, that I plainly see:
But I will never rest, be sure of this,   1495
Till I've got wings and scudded through the air.
[*Exit Kinesias.*
Enter an Informer.
Informer.
Hither as the track I follow,
Certain birds appear in view,

---

chorus dancing round the altar of Bacchus. The poet instructed the chorus provided by the choragus of the tribe, and was hence called *a teacher*, whether of dithyrambic, tragic, or comic poetry. Kinesias says that every tribe vied with the rest in the endeavour to secure him for its *teacher* in dithyrambic contests.

1491—3 (1405—7). Aristophanes often amuses the audience by confounding Cloudcuckooborough with Athens, as here. Leotrophides was a little mite of a man, and therefore a suitable choragus to engage the spare Kinesias. The 'choreutai' best adapted to such employers would be 'flying birds.' (See *The Frogs*, v. 1437, where it is said that Kleokritus winged with Kinesias and borne away by the breezes would be a ludicrous sight.) The tribe to which they belong is given in most editions as 'Kekropida,' the Kekropian, one of the ten Attic tribes. For this word one scholar conjectures 'Kerkopida,' the baboon tribe; but what have the birds to do with baboons? There seems little doubt that Kock's emendation is right, 'Krekopida,' the tribe of the bird krex, on which see v. 1214 (1138), of course suggesting a play of sound between 'Kekropida' and 'Krekopida.'

1498 (1410). "Certain birds, &c." The informer enters singing an air from a song of the Lesbian poet Alkaeus.

Dapplewing'd, without a sou;
O pinionstretching dappled swallow! 1500

Peithetaerus.

This newly-wakened pest is not a light one:
Here comes another fellow trilling airs.

Informer.

O pinionstretching dappled one 'da capo.'

Peithetaerus.

Methinks upon his cloak he sings the catch;
He seems to want no small amount of swallows. 1505

Informer.

Who is't supplies the visitors with wings?

Peithetaerus.

Your humble servant. What are your commands?

Informer.

Wings, wings I want: you need not ask me twice.

Peithetaerus.

Direct to Woolston do you mean to fly?

1504—5 (1416—7). "Upon his cloak." As the informer apostrophizes the swallow twice as *dappled*, Peithetaerus jocularly says he sings about his own cloak, which is *dappled* with patches and holes; and the words added, 'he needs not a few swallows,' allude to the well-known proverb, 'one swallow doesn't make spring-time.'

1509 (1421). "To Woolston:" lit. '*to Pellene.*' Pellene in Achaia was famous for its warm woollen cloaks. These were given as prizes in some of the games. See Pind. *Op.* IX. 98; *Nem.* X. 44.

Informer.
No: but an island-summoner am I,　　　　1510
And an informer.

Peithetaerus.
What a blessed trade!

Informer.
Ay, and a suit-promoter: so I want
A suit of wings to fly about my circuit
And scare the cities with my writs of summons.

Peithetaerus.
With wings you'll summon then more cleverly? 1515

Informer.
No: but, to save annoyance from the pirates,
I'll travel back in the crane caravan,
With many lawsuits swallowed down for ballast.

Peithetaerus.
So that's your business, yours, a strong young man,
To bring vexatious charges against foreigners?　1520

Informer.
What can I do? I never learn'd to dig.

1511 (1423). "Informer," Gr. 'sukophantes.' This well-known Greek word originated in the informations laid against those who exported figs from Attica, in violation of the prohibitory laws. It became the customary name for those who made informing a trade, and was still more generally extended to persons who lived at other people's cost, as parasites. Hence its modern sense, 'sycophant.'

1518 (1429). The allusion here is to the stones supposed to be swallowed by cranes as ballast. See v. 1213 (1137).

Peithetaerus.
But surely there are other decent trades,
In which a fullgrown man might get his bread
By doing rather than perverting justice.

Informer.
Correct me not, but wing me, noble Sir.   1525

Peithetaerus.
I do, by speaking.

Informer.
                Wing by speech? how so?

Peithetaerus.
All men are wing'd by speeches.

Informer.
                    All men?

Peithetaerus.
                            Yes.
Have you not often heard, when to their friends
In barbers' shops the fathers thus discourse:
'Too bad: Dieitrephes has wing'd with talk   1530
That lad of mine to drive his curricle.'
Another says, his boy is all a-wing
For tragedy, and fluttered in his mind.

Informer.
So then by speeches they are wing'd?

1528 (1441). There is some corruption in the Greek here; and by the words '*to their friends*' an emendation is admitted.
1530 (1442). "Dieitrephes." See v. 835 (798).

Peithetaerus.
      They are.   1535
By speeches intellect is elevated
And the man raised aloft. And so would I
Wing you with honest words, and turn you to
A lawful trade.

Informer.
    But I will not be turned.

Peithetaerus.
What will you do then?

Informer.
      Not disgrace my kindred:
Informing's my ancestral occupation.   1540
So fit me with some light and rapid wings,
Falcon's or hawk's, that I may serve my writs
On foreigners, then plead against them here,
Then fly back there again.

Peithetaerus.
     I catch your meaning.
'Tis this: that, ere the foreigner arrives,   1545
He may be cast in damages.

Informer.
    Exactly.

Peithetaerus.
And while he's sailing hither, off you fly
To foreign parts, and seize his goods.

Informer.

You've hit it.
A top's the very thing to be.

Peithetaerus.

A top!
I comprehend; and, by the powers, I've got   1550
These capital wings of Korkyrean make.

Informer.

Woe's me! you've got a whip.

Peithetaerus.

No, no; two wings,
With which I mean this day to set you spinning.
[*Whips him.*

Informer.

Alas, alas!

Peithetaerus.

Come, wing your way from hence
And trickle off, abominable hangdog: 1555
Your justicetwisting tricks shall cost you dear.
[*Exit Informer.*
Now let us gather up the wings and go.
[*Exit Peithetaerus with slaves.*

1555 (1467). Abominable hangdog (O destined to perish most miserably).
1556 (1468). Your, &c. (You shall soon see a bitter justice-perverting roguery).

1551 (1463). "Of Korkyrean make." The whips of Korkyra were famous. That produced here has a double lash.

Chorus.

Many wondrous things and new	*Strophe.*
Come before my gliding view:	
Many very startling sights	1560
We have noticed in our flights.	
From the common road apart,	
At some distance beyond Hart,	
Stands a tree beheld by us,	
And its name Kleonymus:	1565
Fearful 'tis and tall to see,	
Yet a good-for-nothing tree.	
In the springtime when it grows,	
Many a load of figs it shews,	
But in winter on the fields	1570
Its branches shed not leaves but shields.	
There's a region far away,	*Antistrophe.*

1558 (1470), &c. Many wondrous &c. (many things both new and wondrous ere now flew we too, and beheld strange things. For there is a tree growing out of the way, farther off than Kardia, Kleonymus, good for nothing, but merely timid and tall. This in spring ever sprouts and shews figs (lays informations), but in winter again sheds shields for leaves).

1558 (1474), &c. A choric ode dividing Episodes, as here (and twice afterwards), is technically called a Stasimon. This Stasimon has both strophe and antistrophe, but the other two correspond to each other as strophe and antistrophe.

1563 (1474). "At some distance beyond Hart;" *lit. 'farther off than Kardia.'* There is a play on words here. Kardia (Heart) was a town in the Thracian Chersonese. Kleonymus is branded as wanting courage, without 'heart.' He is represented by a tree, goodlooking but worthless. It 'shews figs indeed in spring-time,' that is, in peace he lays base informations (as Kleonymus did during the process of the Hermokopidae); but its winter droppings are shields not leaves; that is, in war-time he plays the coward.

Where our pinions seldom stray,
Unto Nightland's borders near,
In Nolightland's desert drear.　　　　　　　1575
There the children of mankind
Often have with heroes din'd,
And with heroes can abide,
Only not at eventide;
At that season 'twould not be　　　　　　　1580
Safe to keep their company.
If at night mortal wight
Doth upon Orestes light,
Hero bold, he's stript by him,
And smitten in each noble limb.　　　　　　1585

Enter PROMETHEUS *disguised, and under a sunshade.*

Prometheus.

Me miserable! mind Zeus see me not!
Is Peithetaerus in?

1583 (1491). "Orestes." This footpad (see v. 749) is called 'a hero,' as having the same name with the son of Agamemnon. There is an allusion here to a current superstition that a sudden vision of a deity or hero would cause an apoplectic stroke.

1586 (1494), &c. The fourth Episode introduces Prometheus, who has stolen out of heaven disguised, and hiding under a sunshade. He comes to give secret information that the gods, reduced by hunger, are sending an embassy to treat for peace: and he suggests to Peithetaerus what terms he should demand, in order to secure supreme dominion for himself and the bird-realm. The whole scene is a broad caricature of the Promethean myth, as exhibited by Aeschylus in his extant drama, *Prometheus Bound*, and, as we may certainly believe, in the *Fire-bringing Prometheus* (a satyric drama), and the *Prometheus Released*, which are lost.

Peithetaerus re-entering.
Hilloa! who's here?
What wraps are these?

Prometheus.
D'ye spy some god behind me?

Peithetaerus.
Not I, upon my honour! Who are you?

Prometheus.
Inform me then what time o' day it is.   1590

Peithetaerus.
What time o' day? The early afternoon.
But who are you?

Prometheus.
Towards four o'clock, or later?

Peithetaerus.
Your folly sickens me.

Prometheus.
What's Zeus about?
Clearing the clouds off, or collecting them?

Peithetaerus.
A mischief to you.

1592 (1500). "Towards four o'clock:" Gr. 'boulutos,' the *time of loosing kine* from the plough, about four in the afternoon. See Hom. *Il.* XVI. 779. *Od.* IX. 58.

Prometheus.

      Well then, I'll unveil.   1595
      [*throws off his disguise.*

Peithetaerus.

Prometheus, my dear friend!

Prometheus.

      Stop, stop, don't shout.

Peithetaerus.

Why not?

Prometheus.

    Be quiet; don't call out my name,
I'm lost for ever if Zeus view me here.
But, while I'm telling you the news from heaven,
Just take this sunshade, will you? hold it up   1600
Above my head, that so the gods mayn't see me.

Peithetaerus.

Bravissimo! a good device indeed,
Of true Promethean fancy! Come, be quick,
Step under, and then speak without alarm.

    1595 (1503). "I'll unveil." Peithetaerus, provoked by the cross-questioning of Prometheus, begins to revile, upon which, as if replying to the most friendly solicitation, Prometheus discovers himself.

    1602 (1511). "A good, &c:" lit. '*well devised and Promethically.*' Aeschylus says: 'All arts to mortals from Prometheus come.' The name implies *precaution* or *forethought*.

Prometheus.
Now listen with attention.

Peithetaerus.
    Speak: I listen.   1605

Prometheus.
Well! Zeus is ruined.

Peithetaerus.
    Can you date his ruin?

Prometheus.
From your first atmospheric settlement.
No man from that time offers anything
To gods; no savour comes to us on high
From legs of mutton: mulcted of our victims, 1610
We fast as in the Thesmophorian days:
And wild with hunger the barbarian gods,

1610 (1517). Legs of mutton (thigh-meat).

1611 (1519). "In the Thesmophorian days." The Thesmophoria were solemnized by married women in honour of Demeter from the 9th to the 13th of Pyanepsion (November). One of these was a day of mourning and fasting, and abstinence was also required in preparation for the mysteries celebrated during the festival. See *The Thesmophoriazusae* of our poet.

1612 (1520). "The barbarian gods." As barbarous tribes dwell to the north of Greece, so Aristophanes ludicrously supposes barbarous gods existing above the heavenly Olympus, and gives them a title taken from one of the fiercest and most uncivilized Thracian tribes, the Triballi. See Thuk. II. 96. This conception, as shewn here and in the subsequent scene, is one of the raciest humour.

All screeching like Illyrians, fiercely say
They'll march their armies from above on Zeus,
Unless he'll open all the ports, that tripe   1615
And sausages may enter duty-free.

Peithetaerus.

How? are there other and barbarian gods
Above yourselves?

Prometheus.

What are they but barbarians,
Whence Exekestides obtains his siregod?

Peithetaerus.

And these barbarian gods, what is their name?   1620

Prometheus.

Their name? Triballi.

Peithetaerus.

Oh, I understand:
That means to say, they are a 'tribe allied.'

1615 (1524). That tripe, &c. (that chopped entrails may be imported).
1622 (1530). That means, &c. (hence then came *the phrase*, be thou smashed).

1619 (1527). "Siregod." The members of a ward worshipped a common Zeus and Apollo with the title 'siregod' (patrôos). Exekestides, stigmatized by Aristophanes as a spurious citizen, would have no true Hellenic 'siregod,' but must find one among barbarian deities. See vv. 11. 804 (765).

1622 (1530). "A tribe allied." This *jeu de mots* is substituted for that of Aristophanes, which would be lost in literal translation.

Prometheus.

Just so. But let me state one certain fact:
From Zeus and those Triballians up above
Envoys are coming here to treat for peace: 1625
But don't conclude on any terms but these:
That Zeus restore the sceptre to the Birds,
And give you Royalty to be your bride.

Peithetaerus.

Who is this Royalty?

Prometheus.

A lovely maid,
Who has the charge of Zeus's lightning-closet 1630
And all his other stores, his maxims sage,
His wholesome laws, his temperance, his dockyards,
His slang, his paymaster, his sixpences.

1630 (1538). Lightning-closet (lightning).

1629 (1536). "Royalty:" Gr. 'Basileia.' The kingly power of Zeus is personified under this title.

1630 (1538). "Has the charge of." Holden has a reading, not here adopted, giving the sense '*moulds* the lightning.'

1633 (1541). "His slang." Kock, following Reiske, argues in favour of reading 'his ambrosia,' but he does not edit so. There is much weight in what is urged: but the change is too bold. The four things last named here, dockyards &c., are comically taken from Athenian institutions.

"Paymaster:" Gr. 'kolakretes:' an officer who had charge of the fund from which payments were made to jurymen, whose fee would be 'three obols' a day, 'triôbolon,' $4\frac{1}{2}d.$, here called in round numbers 'sixpence.'

Peithetaerus.

Why, then she keeps his all.

Prometheus.

　　　　　　　　She really does: 1634
And when you've got her from him, you've got all.
'Twas for that reason that I came to tell you:
I've always been a zealous friend to men.

Peithetaerus.

True; you're the only god through whom we grill.

Prometheus.

And all the gods, you're well aware, I hate.

Peithetaerus.

Yes, this cleaves to you ever, hate of gods.　　1640

Prometheus.

A genuine Timon! But I must run back;

1638 (1546). "We grill." One offence of Prometheus against Zeus was that he stole fire from heaven, and gave it to men. Aeschylus says: 'Giver of fire to men you see Prometheus.' And Horace; C. I. 3, 'Audax Iapeti genus ignem fraude mala gentibus intulit.'

1641 (1548—9). Kock assigns the words "A genuine Timon" to Peithetaerus. This can hardly be right for the following reason. In v. 1640 (1548) Peithetaerus uses a word designedly ambiguous, which indeed more correctly signifies 'hated of the gods' than 'hating the gods.' If he then added the words 'a genuine Timon,' he would only cancel his own joke, for Timon was '*a man-hater*' only, as Prometheus is '*a god-hater.*' Prometheus is supposed to ignore the cavil, and to accept the phrase of Peithetaerus in his own sense: hence he calls himself a Timon, one who hates

So hand me here the sunshade, that, if Zeus
From upper realms behold me, I may seem
To follow in due form the basket-bearer. 1644

Peithetaerus.

There! take this campstool also for your purpose.
[*Exit Prometheus.*

Chorus.

Near the Shadowfeet are certain shoals, *Strophe.*
Where the dirty Sokrates charms souls.

1645 (1552). There! take, &c. (and take this stool and be a stool-bearer).

---

his fellow-gods as truly as Timon did his fellow-men. The story of Timon the misanthrope, son of Echekrates, is so well known from Shakspeare's play, that it need not be related here.

1644-5 (1551—2). In the procession of the Panathenaea the sacred baskets were borne by Athenian maidens, daughters of citizens, on their heads. Such a maiden was called 'Basket-bearer' (kanephoros). Behind each walked the daughter of a resident alien (metoikos) with a sunshade to protect the basket-bearer from sun or rain, and a campstool (diphros) on which she could rest when fatigued. Such a maiden was called 'a stool-bearer' (diphrophoros); and Prometheus hopes to be taken by Zeus for one of these.

1646 (1553), &c. This Stasimon and its antistrophe after Episode V. are a sequel to the one at v. 1558 (1470), introducing, in the same manner, scenes and characters supposed to have been viewed by the Birds in their flights: but really such as Aristophanes selects for ridicule. In this place the chief hero is Peisander: but occasion is taken to caricature again the poet's old *bête noire,* Sokrates, with his friend Chaerephon. Readers of Thirlwall's and Grote's histories are acquainted with the unprincipled character and conduct of this Peisander, an inquisitor in the affair of the Hermo-

The spirit that left his living frame
To gaze at there, Peisander came,
Camel-lamb as victim carried,   1650
Cut its throat, and near it tarried,

kopidae, B.C. 415, Archon in 414, afterwards (for his traitorous conduct in the oligarchic conspiracy of 411) condemned to death, but saved by flight. His tall ungainly form (like a camel's), his credulity and his cowardice, are here ridiculed. The poet uses the current superstition that the souls of the dead could be evoked by sacrifice and prayer, and be seen and questioned by the living. Passing by the scriptural narrative of the Witch of Endor, the earliest classical instance is that of Odysseus in Hom. *Od.* XI. 49, here cited. Such exorcism was practised in establishments on the banks of lakes and rivers, as at Avernus in Italy, and on the Acheron in Thesprotia. See Herod. V. 92. These were called 'psychopompeia,' or, when used for divination, 'psychomanteia.' Sokrates is exorcist, partly on account of his personal eccentricities, partly because he 'charmed the souls' of his disciples. One of these, the ghostlike Chaerephon, nicknamed the bat (see v. 1377), is chosen as the soul that appears to Peisander, because his enthusiastic temper was capable of supplying to the cowardly politician that which had 'left his living frame,' a brave 'spirit,' perhaps also because his own visage might gain some colour from the blood of the 'camel-lamb.' Thus the pale-faced but warm-hearted young philosopher is contrasted with the ruddy but spiritless political intriguer.

    1646 (1553). "Shadow-feet:" Gr. 'Skiapodes.' Pliny (N. H. VII. 2) cites an absurd account given by Ctesias of a Libyan people, one-legged, with feet so enormous as so serve them for sunshades while they sleep: hence their name, Skiapodes.

    1650 (1559). "Camel-lamb." The slaughter of sheep in the process of exorcism is described by Homer. The lamb here mentioned is called a camel-lamb, in ridicule of Peisander's size.

    1651 (1561). "And near it tarried." The MS. reading gives 'and went away.' This (as Kock observes) can hardly be true: for Peisander waits to see the spirit (Chaerephon) come up, and

As Odysseus did of old:
Suddenly from beneath the mould,
Of the camel's blood to sup,
He saw Chaerephon the bat come up.   1655

SCENE II. *Part of the ramparts of Cloudcuckooborough; an alcove in the scene as a kitchen where* PEITHE-TAERUS *is engaged with slaves cooking. Enter* POSEIDON, HERAKLES *and* TRIBALLUS.

Poseidon.

This is the fortress of Cloudcuckooborough
Within our view, to which we're sent as envoys.
What's that you're doing there? pulling your cloak

Odysseus in Homer says, 'We *sat*, and up there came my mother's spirit.'

1654 (1562). "Camel's blood." The Gr. word used (laima) has no existence: but we may suppose it to be a coinage of the poet, hybrid between 'laimos,' *throat*, and 'haima' *blood*: i.e. *throat-blood*.

1656 (1565), &c. The three ambassadors from heaven arrive; Poseidon, Herakles and a Triballian God. They find Peithetaerus engaged in preparations for a banquet: and although Herakles comes with a murderous purpose, the savour of the kitchen and the promise of a good meal persuade him to accept the conditions of Peithetaerus. He gets the vote of the Triballian also; and, in spite of Poseidon's opposition, the sceptre and the maiden are conceded. They then retire with Peithetaerus, proposing to take him with them back to heaven, where Royalty, with her belongings, shall be delivered to the Bird-chief in person. Schönborn's view is (*die Skene der Hellenen* p. 321), that a change of scene has been effected before the arrival of the envoys. It seems more likely that this would be done, if at all, during the longer Stasimon at v. 1558 (1470). His opinion, however, is here accepted.

1658 (1567). The Triballian, whose personal appearance, no doubt, corresponds to his title of barbarian, is unacquainted with

To the left side in that ungainly style? 1659
Put round and draw it, can't you? to the right.
Ah, clumsy being! you're a born Laispodias.

[*To the Triballian God.*

What will you bring us to, Democracy,
If the gods choose a deputy like this?
Be still, you plague! Of all the gods I've seen
You are the one most barbarous by far. 1665

[*To the Triballian again.*

Well, Herakles, what's to be done?

Herakles.

You've heard,
I want to strangle him outright, the man,
Whoe'er he is, that's walling out the gods.

---

the style of wearing the cloak (himation) which is fashionable at Olympus, as in Athens. This fashion was, to pass it over the left shoulder, draw it round the back towards the right (epi dexia), and passing it under the right arm, which was left free, then to bring it back to the left shoulder, where it was finally clasped, hanging down gracefully towards the feet. The clumsy Triballian has put on his cloak the reverse way, towards the left (ep' aristera), shewing himself thoroughly *gauche* and illbred. This draws on him the wrath and rebuke of the high-bred Olympian, Poseidon.

1661 (1569). "Laispodias:" a commander mentioned by Thuk. VI. 105, and again VIII. 86, as one of the oligarchic faction. The Scholiast says that he wore his cloak in an unusual way to hide a defect in his legs. But the name may perhaps be used merely for the sake of its etymology, 'left-footed,' implying awkwardness.

1662 (1570). The bad choice of an envoy is laughably ascribed to democratic institutions adopted in Olympus.

1664 (1572). "Be still." This is certainly said by Poseidon, who sees that his clumsy colleague, attempting to reverse his cloak, only makes matters worse.

Poseidon.

Nay, Sir, but our instructions are to treat   1669
For peace.

Herakles.

So much the more I vote for strangling.

Peithetaerus.

Hand the cheese-scraper, somebody: fetch silphium;
Bring cheese, and heat the coals within the grate.

Poseidon.

We bid the gentleman good day, we gods,
Three in commission.

Peithetaerus.

Now then, scrape the silphium.

Herakles.

What meat is this you're dressing?

Peithetaerus.

                      Certain birds
Against the democratic birds arose,   1676
And suffered condemnation for high treason.

1671 (**1578**). Peithetaerus here baits the hook for Herakles, whose character as a gourmand had been thoroughly established by Euripides in his *Alkestis*.

1674 (1582). Here and elsewhere Peithetaerus affects supreme indifference to the presence of the deities, and devotion to his own culinary duties.

1675 (1583). Herakles begins to nibble at the bait.

Herakles.
So then, you first scrape silphium on them, do you?

Peithetaerus.
Ah, Herakles, good morning. What's your pleasure?

Poseidon.
We're come as envoys from the gods to treat   1680
About a termination of the war.

Peithetaerus.
There's not a drop of oil within the cruse.

Herakles.
And yet your volaille wants a nice rich sauce.

Poseidon.
We for our part gain nothing by the war,
And you, by being friendly with the gods,   1685
Would have rain-water in your tanks at once,
And live without cessation halcyon days.
On all these points we bring full powers to treat.

Peithetaerus.
Well; we were not the first in former time
To war with you: and, now, if so resolved,   1690
And if at last you're willing to do justice,
We'll come to terms. Our just demand is this,
That Zeus restore the sceptre to us birds.
And if we settle things on this condition,
I shall invite the embassy to luncheon.   1695

1695 (1602). "To luncheon." Peithetaerus here spins his bait so temptingly, that Herakles gorges it without further hesitation.

Herakles.
I'm quite content with this, and give my vote—

Poseidon.
For what, you madman? You're a silly glutton:
You'll rob your father of his royal sway?

Peithetaerus.
So, so? and won't you gods be stronger far
If birds command below? For mortals now   1700
Conceal'd beneath the clouds hang down their heads,
And call on you to witness perjuries.
But, if you have the birds for your allies,
When by the raven and by Zeus a man
Shall swear, and break his plight, the raven then, 1705
Approaching unperceiv'd, shall pounce on him,
And strike his eye out with a single blow.

Poseidon.
Ay, by Poseidon, this at least's well said.

Herakles.
I think so.

Poseidon.
What do you say?
[*To the Triballian.*
Triballian.
Nabaisatreu.

1708 (1604). Poseidon ludicrously adjures himself.
1709 (1615). "Nabaisatreu." Kock takes this to mean *let us*

Peithetaerus.

You see, he gives assent. Hear furthermore   1710
How great a service we've in store for you.
If any man shall vow to any god
A sacrifice, and then with artful quibbles
Excuse himself and say, 'The gods can wait,'
Declining from mere stinginess to pay,   1715
This also we'll exact.

Poseidon.
      How so? let's see.

Peithetaerus.

When the man's counting out a petty sum,
Or sitting in his bath, a kite shall swoop
Unnotic'd, clutch the coins, and carry up
The value of two sheep unto the god.   1720

Herakles.
I vote for giving back the sceptre to them.

Poseidon.
Ask the Triballian next.

---

three go back, a virtually negative reply, which Peithetaerus pretends to interpret otherwise. He proceeds, however, to give a second instance in favour of concession.

   1723 (1628). Instead of asking the Triballian if he votes for yielding, Herakles banteringly asks, if he votes for 'smarting,' that is, accepting bad terms. The Triballian's reply is in Aristophanes 'saunaka baktarikrousa,' which is partly intelligible; 'beat with the stick my (skin?).' An analogous jargon is substituted in the version.

Herakles.
Do you, Triballian,
Consent to a sound whipping?

Triballian.
Stikaliki
Mitaki.

Herakles.
My proposal's good, he says.

Poseidon.
If you both vote so, then I vote with you.   1725

Herakles.
Sir, we concede this point about the sceptre.

Peithetaerus.
Ay, but there's one thing more which I forgot.
Hera indeed I yield to Zeus, but he
Must give the Princess Royalty to me
In lawful wedlock.

Poseidon.
Peace is not your object: 1730
Let us go home again.

Peithetaerus.
Little I care.
Cook, mind you make the sauce sweet.

1727 (1632). Peithetaerus has skilfully obtained the concession of one claim before he puts forward the other, which he pretends to recollect suddenly.

Herakles.

                        My good man
Poseidon, whither are you rushing off?
Are we to go to war about one woman?

Poseidon.
What must we do then?

Herakles.
           Come to terms of course.   1735

Poseidon.
Poor wretch, you know not that you're being duped.
You harm yourself moreover. If Zeus die,
After the kingdom has been given to these,
You will be poor: for all the money's yours
That Zeus will leave behind him at his death.

Peithetaerus.
O dear, O dear! how sadly he deceives you!   1741
Come here aside, and have a word with me.
Your uncle sets you wrong, unhappy Sir;
Not one hair's breadth of all your father's goods
Is yours by law. You're illegitimate.   1745

Herakles.
I illegitimate? What can you mean?

    1732 (1638). "My good man." The gods comically address one another with human familiarity.

    1739 (1644). "The money's yours." This and all that follows is highly comic. Zeus, the supreme and immortal deity, is supposed to be going to die some day, and leave money behind him which will be inherited by the rules of Attic law.

Peithetaerus.

You are, by Zeus! a foreign woman's child:
Or how d'ye think Athene could be heiress,
A daughter, had she lawful brothers living?

Herakles.

Well, but suppose my sire give me the money 1750
After his death, by special codicil,
As to a spurious son.

Peithetaerus.

    The law forbids him.
Why, this Poseidon, who's now cramming you,
Will be the first to claim your father's money,
Saying that he himself is lawful brother. 1755
I'll now recite to you the law of Solon:

'A bastard shall have no inheritance while lawful children are alive, and, if there are no lawful children, then the next of kin shall share the property between them.' 1760

Herakles.

So then I've no claim to my father's money?

1752 (1656). "The law forbids him." Peithetaerus, while asserting that the simple Herakles is duped by his uncle Poseidon, does not however tell him the exact truth. If a father died intestate, illegitimate children at Athens took nothing. But the father could bequeath them a limited sum: he could also, during his life, legitimate them, by obtaining the consent of the people, and presenting them, as adopted, to his wardsmen for enrolment. Zeus however had not done this, says Peithetaerus in his comic vein; therefore Herakles, not having been legitimately adopted, will be left penniless.

Peithetaerus.

No, none, by Zeus. Just tell me, did your father
At any time present you to his wardsmen?

Herakles.

Me? never: I'd been wondering at it long.

Peithetaerus.

Why stare up at the sky with looks like cudgels?
Stand on our side, and I'll create you king,   1766
I'll give you bird's milk to your heart's content.

Herakles.

Again what you propose, I think, is just
About the maiden, and I yield her to you.

Peithetaerus.

And what say you?   [*To Poseidon.*

Poseidon.

    I vote the other way.   1770

Peithetaerus.

All rests with the Triballian. What say you?
                                          [*To the Triballian.*

Triballian.

Dipritti girli biggi royalbaki
Abirdi yieldimi.

    1765 (1671). Herakles looks up as if he would like to knock his father down: and Peithetaerus, promising him a kingdom and —bird's milk withal, catches his silly fish a second time.

    1772 (1679). The barbaric Greek of the Triballian is quite intelligible, and is here translated into barbarous English, meaning ' the pretty maiden and great kingdom I yield back to the birds.'

Herakles.

He says he yields.

Poseidon.

No, no! he does not really say he yields,
But only twitters as the swallows do.   1775

Peithetaerus.

Why, then he says he yields her to the swallows.

Poseidon.

Well, draw your clauses, and arrange between you:
For, since you're both agreed, I'll say no more.

Herakles.

Our vote is, to admit all your conditions.
But come with us to heaven yourself: there take 1780
The Princess Royalty and all her trousseau.

Peithetaerus.

In seasonable time then for the wedding
These birds were slaughtered.

Herakles.

    Will you let me stay
Meantime and roast this meat, while you depart? 1784

1775 (1682). "As the swallows do." Swallows are the birds whose twittering was especially considered by the Greeks to resemble the language of barbarian nations. See Aesch. *Ag.* 1050 and *The Frogs*, vv. 93, 681.

Poseidon.

You roast the meat? much tasting's what you mean.
Come on with us.

Herakles.

I should have been in clover.

Peithetaerus.

Let some one get me out a wedding-mantle.
[*Exeunt Peithetaerus and the three gods.*

Chorus. *Antistrophe.*

In the Peachings, on the Waterglass side,
Rascally tonguebellied tribes abide,

1785 (1691). "Much tasting." The Gr. word (tentheia) answers in some measure to the French '*gourmandise*,' implying the selection of the nicest dainties in eating.

1786 (1692). "I should have been in clover." Kock supposes Herakles to say ironically, 'I should be well off if I went with you to heaven' where there is nothing to eat. Surely this is erroneous on grounds of logic and language. Peithetaerus has given no consent: the presence of the three envoys would be required in the council of Olympus: and it is far more comic to understand that the disappointed glutton, following his colleagues, casts a longing lingering look at the *matelote* he leaves behind, and mutters, 'how nice it *would have been*.' The promised luncheon seems to be deferred to the marriage celebration. Comedy does not care for the famous unities.

1788 (1696), &c. In this antistrophic Stasimon the objects of ridicule are the foreign 'Sophists' who travelled about lecturing and teaching rhetoric for money. Two of these are especially named, (1) the famous Gorgias of Leontini in Sicily, and (2) Philippus, a rhetorician of the same school. He is called in *The Wasps* (v. 421) 'son of Gorgias,' perhaps not in the literal sense. They are termed *tongue-bellied* (ventriloquists), because they lived

[Exodos.] THE BIRDS.

Who with their tongues both reap and sow,   1790
And grapes and figs in plenty grow.
These are of barbarian races,
Philips all and Gorgiases.
Hence arose a custom new,
To those tonguebellied Philips due: 1795
Attic usage everywhere
Cuts the tongue for a separate share.

Enter Third Messenger.

Third Messenger.
O ye of every countless good possest,

---

by lecturing. They are said to reside at 'Phanae' (here rendered *the Peachings*), a comically invented name: implying that the rhetoric taught by these sophists enabled rascally 'informers' to make the worse appear the better reason. The words 'on the Waterglass side' (Gr. Klepsydra) point (1) to the fountain of Klepsydra ('hiding water') on the slope of the Akropolis, (2) to the implement so called, the Waterglass, by which the time allowed for speeches in courts of law was measured.

1791 (1699). "Figs." An allusion to the informers (sycophants lit. 'figshewers').

1792 (1700). "Barbarian:" here 'non-Athenian': for Leontini was a Hellenic colony, where Greek was spoken.

1797 (1705). "Cuts the tongue." Aristophanes plays false with antiquarian lore when it suits him. In the Homeric age the tongues of victims were reserved, and offered to the gods with a libation after the banquet. See Hom. *Od.* III. 332, 341. Some say this was in honour of Hermes, god of eloquence. At Athens, in some sacrifices, the tongue became the perquisite of the heralds in attendance: of whom Hermes was the tutelar god. See *The Peace*, v. 1060, *Plutus*, v. 1110. It seems, especially from the former passage, as if the herald gave formal notice to the sacrificing priest with the words, 'the tongue is cut separately.'

1798 (1706), &c. Here begins the Exodos or concluding scene.

O flying race of birds, supremely blest,
Receive the monarch in his prosperous home.   1800
He comes, he comes: like him in goldbright dome
Ne'er dawn'd to view the full-orb'd glittering star:
No beamy splendour of the sun from far
Shone forth so glorious as the queenly bride
Of untold beauty moving by his side.   1805
Flashing the wingèd levin-bolt of Jove
He comes, while soars to vaulted skies above
A scent unutterable, beauteous sight,
And incense-breezes coil a smoky light.
Himself appears: the goddess Muse to-day   1810
Behoves from holy lips to pour the auspicious lay.

PEITHETAERUS *and* BASILEIA *descend in a flying car, while the Chorus sings.*

Chorus.
Room for the company! cheerily, merrily

The messenger is supposed to have attended Peithetaerus to heaven, and to announce his return as an avant-courier. His speech is a parody of the most inflated tragic style. The Chorus prepare to receive Peithetaerus, who descends from Olympus in a chariot with Basileia (Royalty), as 'the Zeus' of the Birds. All the resources of the Attic stage were evidently employed to produce a grand effect to eye and ear in this concluding scene. First comes the hymeneal song of the Chorus; then lightning and thunder accompany their exultant hymn of praise. Finally the bride and bridegroom ascend to the 'hall of Zeus,'—the cloud-palace where their wedding is to be celebrated—amidst the crash of musical instruments and the Paean shouts raised by the Birds to their 'supremest deity.'

    1802 (1710). "The full-orb'd glittering star": i.e. 'the full moon.'
    1812 (1720). "Cheerily, merrily." The Greek here could not be literally rendered with any corresponding effect. These adverbs

THE BIRDS.

Flutter around him,
Wishing him joy of the joy that has crown'd him!
O bliss! O bliss! 1815
What bloom of youth, what beauty this!
   To the city of thy sway
Happy is thy marriage day.
Great fortune for the Birds is stor'd,
Yea, great, through this victorious lord. 1820
So with Hymen's songs of glee
And bridal carols welcome ye
Him and his partner Royalty.

SONG I.

   When the goddess Fates allied   *Strophe.*
   To Hera, his Olympian bride,   1825
   Him, the high and heavenly One,
   Him who held the exalted throne,
They sang the song of Hymen Hymenaeus.

   Golden-wing'd, the bloomy Love   *Antistrophe.*
   His chariot lightly reining drove,   1830
   With his present power to bless
   Jove's and Hera's happiness,
And sang the song of Hymen Hymenaeus.

Peithetaerus.

Your lays they are sprightful, your music delightful,
Your language is striking, and quite to my liking. 1835

---

partly take the place of four Imperative verbs (anage, dieche, parage, pareche) which bid the crowd make room, expand themselves and form a double line for the passage of Peithetaerus, his bride, and their train.

Chorus.

Stay yet a little while and sing
  The earth-descending crashes,
  The fiery-gleaming flashes,
The terrible white bolt of Zeus the king.

Song II.

O the mighty golden blaze of lightning!   1840
O the flamy spear of Zeus immortal!
O the hoarsely-echoed peals of thunder
Swelling all the cloudy vault from under,
And the rush of rain from heaven's high portal!
Now with these our chief the earth is fright'ning.
All the power of Jove he comes possessing;   1846
Royalty, who in glory splendid
On the ancient throne of Zeus attended,
He brings by his side in stately pride,
His queen, his bride, his blessing.   1850
Sing we the song of Hymen Hymenaeus!

Peithetaerus.

Haste ye the wedding-hour to grace,   *Strophe.*
All my mates of feathered race:
Up to the hall of Jove ascend;
There the bridal couch attend.   1855

    1842—50 (1750—3). "O the hoarsely......blessing." The original is of necessity expanded here with much freedom. Lit. *O earth-going deep-sounding and likewise rain-bringing thunders, with which this man now shakes earth. Having become master of all that was Jove's, he possesses also Royalty, assessor of Zeus.*

Reach me thy hand, O blessèd one,   *Antistrophe.*
Our procession is begun;
And, as thy floating form I stay,
Grasp my pinions, and away!

[*The procession goes* forth amidst jubilant music.

Chorus.

Taralala, lalala!   1860
Waft the conqueror, waft on high,
Thrilling lyre and Paean-cry!
Taralala, lalala!
Hail to thee, all hail to thee,
Our supremest deity!   1865

1862 (1764). "Thrilling lyre:" The Greek word (ténella) is often used in imitation of the twanging sound of lyre or guitar.

1865 (1765). On the parts severally taken by Peithetaerus, the Chorus and the Coryphaeus in this Exodos, see Supplementary Notes.

APPENDICES.

APPENDIX A.

Parabasis Proper.

In THE CLOUDS the Parabasis proper is in the peculiar metre invented by Eupolis, and thence called Eupolidean: being without a 'pnigos.' In *The Frogs* the Parabasis proper with its 'pnigos' is omitted. The *Lysistrata, Ecclesiazusae* and *Plutus* have no Parabasis. But in the other extant comedies of Aristophanes, *The Acharnians*, *The Knights*, *The Wasps*, *The Peace*, *The Birds*, and *The Thesmophoriazusae*, the Parabasis proper is in the metre called Anapaestic Tetrameter Catalectic. This was so usual that in three of these plays we find this portion of the play called 'the Anapaests.' A version of the passage in its original rhythm is therefore added here as instructive, while in the text the rhymed Trochaic has been introduced as more agreeable to a modern ear and more accordant to the general character of the present work.

vv. 720—761 (685—722).

Ho ye men who by nature are dim-lived, attend, ye most semblant of all to the leaf-race,
Little furnish'd with strength, and mere figments of clay, shadow-wrought population and nerveless;
O ye wingless ephemerals, born to endure, O ye men that are mortal and dreamlike,
Unto us the immortals give diligent heed, unto us who are ever existent,
The etherial dwellers, untouch'd by old age, the devisers of plans never-ending:

That, when once ye have learnt all the lore that we teach of
   the regions above so veracious,
When ye know to the full the true nature of birds, the descent
   of the gods, and the rivers
That through Chaos and Erebus run, ye may bid prosy Prodikus
   hang for the future.
First Chaos and Night and black Erebus were, and grim Tarta-
   rus widely extended;
But at that time nor Earth was in being, nor Air, nor the Hea-
   ven itself was existing,
When in Erebus' limitless lap first of all did the dark-plumed
   Night lay a wind-egg,
Whence in due revolution of seasons sprang Love, the dispenser
   of all that is sweetest,
With his pinions of gold shining brightly behind, and in speed
   like to wind-rolling eddies.
He in Tartarus wide, as the legend imports, with the dark misty
   Chaos uniting,
Became father of us; and there nurtured our race, till we came
   forth to light for the first time.
There existed no race of immortals until Love wrought to the
   blending of all things;
But, when one with another was mingled, arose the great heaven,
   the earth and the ocean,
And the stock never-dying of all happy gods. Thus of all
   blessed beings we're oldest.
Many facts prove us children of Love; for we fly, and are fond
   of consorting with lovers,
Who, when other resources are fruitless, have found that the gift
   of a bird is effective,
And the battle of love may be won by a quail, or a goose, or a
   finch or a sparrow.
Of the many great blessings that mortals enjoy, those they get
   from the birds are the greatest.
In the first place of seasons the signals we bring, of the winter,
   the spring and the summer.

They must sow when the clangour is heard in the air of the crane into Libya retreating;
At the same time he tells the ship-captain to hang up the rudder and tranquilly slumber,
And he bids for Orestes be woven a cloak, lest he shiver and take to dismantling.
The next bird after this that appears is the kite, introducing a different season,
When the spring-laden fleece of the sheep must be shorn: then the swallow next makes her appearance,
Who declares it is time to dispose of the cloak and to purchase a blouse for the dogdays.
Furthermore we are Ammon and Delphi to you, your Dodona, your Phoebus Apollo;
For ye come to the birds first of all for advice, ere ye go to your worldly vocations,
To your commerce in marts, to the choice of a trade, and another, it may be, to marriage.
Whatsoever about divination decides, with the title of bird ye endow it;
Ye pronounce it 'a bird,' be it oracle, sneeze, voice or omen or footman or donkey.
So this question we ask, and the answer is plain; are we not your prophetic Apollo?

APPENDIX B.

*Syllabus of the most important various readings of the Greek Text
followed in the Translation.*

[The initials express B. Bergk, H. Holden, K. Kock, M. Meineke.]

23. τί δ' ἡ κορώνη; τῆς ὁδοῦ τι λέγει πέρι; conj. (MSS. have οὐδ' or ἦ δ' ἤ): τί δ'; ἡ κορώνη τῆς κ.τ.λ. Meineke. Holden, with Cobet, omits the first question and the τι before λέγει.

75—6. οὗτός γ' ἄτ', οἶμαι,...ὦν· ὅτε μὲν ἐρᾷ κ.τ.λ. M. &c.

150. ὁτιὴ νὴ τοὺς θεοὺς ὅσ' οὐκ ἰδών, Kock, who justly says that ὁτιή as a repeated question (for ὁτιὴ τί; or ὁτιὴ τί δή) is inadmissible. In Holden's text (Ed. 2) and in M., νὴ τοὺς θεοὺς ὅτι for ὅτι νὴ τοὺς θεούς is questionable. H. should have kept ὅσ', which he claims as his own conjecture. K. ascribes it to Bothe.

168. τίς ἐστιν οὗτος; Dobree, (vulg. τίς ὄρνις οὗτος;).

169. ἄνθρωπος ὄρνις ἀστάθμητος πετόμενος. M. H.

177. In all modern editions this line is written ἀπολαύσομαί τι δ' εἰ διαστραφήσομαι. The ordinary construction of ἀπολαύω is with Accus. and Gen. (τί τινος); but the Accus. may be omitted; and for the Gen. a Participle may stand, as v. 1358 of this play, ἀπέλαυσα τἄρα νὴ Δί' ἐλθὼν ἐνθαδί, which is followed by a condition (as in 177), εἴπερ γέ μοι καὶ τὸν πατέρα βοσκητέον. Considering the awkward form of the words ἀπ. τι δ', the translator offers the conjecture, ἀπολαύσομαι τοῦδ' εἰ διαστραφήσομαι.

192. διὰ τῆς κ.τ.λ. omitted (with almost all editors) as an interpolation from 1218.

213. Ἴτυν ἐλελιζομένης δ' ἱεροῖς μέλεσιν, M. (vulg. Ἴτυν ἐλελιζομένη διεροῖς μέλεσιν).

APPENDIX B.

248-9. ὄρνις πτέρων ποικίλος, M. K. H. (vulg. ὄ. πτεροποίκιλος).
273. εἰκότως γε· καὶ γὰρ ὄνομ' αὐτῷ 'στὶ, Köchly (vulg. εἰκότως. καὶ γὰρ ὄνομ' αὐτῷ γ' ἐστὶ).
276. ἀθροβάτης, Reisig, &c. (vulg. ὀριβάτης).
360. πρὸ σαυτοῦ, Bentley &c. (vulg. πρὸς αὐτόν).
361. προσδοῦ, Haupt (vulg. προσθοῦ).
382. Many conjectures are offered in the place of μάθοι γὰρ ἄν τις κἀπὸ τῶν ἐχθρῶν σοφόν, which merely repeats what the Hoopoe had said v. 375, while the use of σοφόν without article is scarcely tolerable. Perhaps Dobree's μάθοις γὰρ ἄν τι κ.τ.λ. is the simplest correction.
386. Ἡ πρίν, B. (vulg. ἡμῖν).
388. Halbertsma, approved by M., rejects the words τὸν ὀβελίσκον as a gloss. But then what becomes of the metre?
396. The word δημοσίᾳ (vulg.) or δημόσια (Brunck) is difficult here; the former being unmetrical, the latter questionable Greek. Meineke only speaks of some latent corruption, and proposes δημόθεν. The sense, however, is not doubtful.
457. σὺ δὲ τοῦθ' οὕρας λέγ' ἐς κοινόν, M. (vulg. ὁρᾷς): B. ὁ δρᾷς.
465. τρίπαλαι, Cobet, &c. (vulg. τι πάλαι).
467. The conjecture of M., followed by H., τίνος ἡμεῖς; for τίνος;—ὑμεῖς is not convincingly certain.
480. ὡς ἀποδώσει, M. (vulg. οὐκ ἀποδώσει). This conjecture is ascribed by M. to Hamaker, but by H. K. (rightly, no doubt) to Bentley.
484. ἦρχέ τε Περσῶν, πρότερος πάντων Δαρείων καὶ Μεγαβάζων, Haupt (vulg. πρῶτος πάντων Δαρείου καὶ Μεγαβάζου).
492. On Kock's ingenious conjecture ἀποδύσοντες for ὑποδησάμενοι, see footnote. To adopt it would be over-bold: but its plausibility must be admitted.
519. οὗτοι (vulg. αὐτοὶ) by conjecture, Transl. See footnote.
523. νῦν δ' αὖ μανᾶς (vulg. νῦν δ' ἀνδράποδ' ἠλιθίους μανᾶς).
525—6. βάλλουσ' ὑμᾶς κἀν τοῖς ἱεροῖς, πᾶς τις ἐφ' ὑμῖν δ' ὀρνιθευτὴς B. (vulg. βάλλουσ' ὑμᾶς, κἀν τοῖς ἱεροῖς πᾶς τις ἐφ' ὑμῖν ὀρνιθευτὴς).
534—5. Here Hermann's conjecture κατατρίψαντες (for καὶ τρίψαντες) is received by M. H.; and Kock's καταχυσμάτιον (for

APPENDIX B.

κατάχυσμ' ἕτερον) is approved by M.; but neither of these is essential. The καὶ in κἄπειτα is idiomatic in Aristophanes after a participle.

538. αὔων, Reiske (vulg. αὐτῶν).
543. ἐπ' ἐμοῦ (vulg.), ἐπ' ἐμοί, M. with one MS.
567. Here MSS. have θύῃ τις and μελιττοῦτας (for μελιτοῦττας). Brunck introduces βοῦν, spoiling metre. Meineke, followed by H. K., reads ἦν δ' Ἡρακλέει θύῃσι, λάρῳ ναστοὺς θύειν μελιτοῦντας, which the translator follows, yet suspects that θύῃ τι (Bergk) may be more true than θύῃσι.
575. Ἥρην, Bentley (vulg. Ἶριν). βῆναι, M. (vulg. εἶναι).
577. ἡμᾶς (vulg. ὑμᾶς), Köchly, who rightly assigns this and the next half-verse to Peithetaerus.
593. τὰ μέταλλ' (for which Cobet conj. τὰ μὲν ἄλλ'). δείξουσι, B. (vulg. δώσουσι).
604. ὑγίει' αὖ, M. (vulg. ὑγίεια).
632. δίκαιος ἄδολος ὅσιος, B. H. (vulg. δικαίους ἀδόλους ὁσίους).
644. τῳδεδὶ, Dind. (vulg. τῷδε τί;), rightly assigned by Bergk to Peithetaerus.
718. ἄλλος, M. K. H. (vulg. ἀνδρός).
728. ὥραις. K. reads λιαραῖς after Köchly. Hamaker considers the words ἔξετε—πνίγει an interpolation. The translator has ventured to retain them, and to give their general spirit somewhat freely.
857. συναυλείτω δὲ Χαῖρις ᾠδᾷ, Hermann M.K.H. (vulg. συνᾳδέτω δὲ Χαῖρις ᾠδάν).
878. The translator has followed Holden in placing the words καὶ ὄρνισιν Ὀλυμπίοις καὶ Ὀλυμπίῃσι πᾶσι καὶ πάσῃσι before διδόναι κ.τ.λ., but he has no doubt that after ἑστιούχῳ a speech of Peithetaerus and a clause of the liturgy are lost.
881. ἥρωσιν ὄρνισι, Herm. etc. (vulg. ἥρ. καὶ ὄρν.).
886. καὶ ἡρισάλπιγγι, added from the Scholiast by editors.
905. τεαῖς. A neat conjecture of Tyrwhitt is νέαις.
930. τεῶν, Köchly (vulg. τεῖν).
951. νιφοβόλα, M. (vulg. νιφόβολα).
979. οὐ λᾶιος, M. (vulg. οὐδ' αἰετὸς). This ingenious correction

(or some other) is required. Λᾶῖος is a kind of *throstle*, mentioned by Aristotle.

996. κατὰ γύας, Dawes, &c. (vulg. κατ' ἀγυίας).

1001, 1002. προσθεὶς οὖν ἐγὼ τὸν κάνον', ἄνωθεν τουτονὶ τὸν καμπύλον Ἐνθεὶς διαβήτην κ.τ.λ., K. (vulg. comma after καμπύλον, not after κάνον'. Perhaps ἄνω δὲ for ἄνωθεν? Transl.

1013. ξενηλατεῖται, Haupt (vulg. ξενηλατοῦνται). φρένες, K. (vulg. τινές).

1040. τοῖς αὐτοῖς, Hamaker (vulg. τοῖσδε τοῖς).

1041. Meineke and K. would omit καὶ ψηφίσμασι, as the transtion does. B. reads καὶ νομίσμασι, *coins*.

1070. ἐκ φοναῖς ὄλλυται, Reisig, &c. (vulg. φοναῖσιν ἐξόλλυται).

1078. ἢν δὲ ζῶν τις ἀγάγῃ, Dind. M. H. ἢν δὲ ζῶντ' ἄγῃ τις Dobr. (MSS ἐὰν δὲ ζῶντ' ἀγάγῃ).

1081. ἐγχεῖ. Suspected without ground by M. K.

1095. ὀξὺ μέλος, Brunck, &c. (vulg. ὀξυμελὴς).

1131. ἑκατοντορόγυιον, Hotchkis, &c. (vulg. ἑκατοντόργυιον). Mr Leonard Hotchkis, to whom this certain correction is due, was Head-master of Shrewsbury School in the middle of the 18th century.

μάκρους. This, says Meineke, is corrupt. But it cannot be corrected: and may not our poet, among his comic eccentricities, include the coinage of a new word? Holden suggests βάθους.

1150. M. was the first to point out the lacuna here between the words κάτοπιν and ὥσπερ. See footnote. Dobree thinks that the mortar softened by the swallows is compared to the sopped food given by nurses to infants. But surely the case of παιδία (Nom.) suggests that the softening is done by children themselves, as the translation expresses.

1154. ἀπειργάσαντ' ὄρνιθες ;—Ἦσαν κ.τ.λ., Hamaker, (vulg. ἀπειργάσαντ' ;—Ὄρνιθες ἦσαν κ.τ.λ.).

1221. ἀδικεῖς δέ· καὶ νῦν ἀρά γ' οἶσθα κ.τ.λ., Herm. (vulg. ἀδικεῖς δὲ καὶ νῦν· ἀρά γ' κ.τ.λ.).

1228. ἀκροατέ' ὑμῖν, Blaydes, &c. (vulg. ἀκροατέον ὑμῖν).

1234. οἴοισιν; M. (vulg. ποίοισιν;).

1238. δείσας, Porson (vulg. δεινάς).

APPENDIX B.

1272—3. ὦ τρισμακάρι' ὦ κλεινότατ' ὦ γλαφυρώτατε, ὦ κατακέλευσον, κατακέλευσον. M. (from Rav. MS.)

1282. ἐσωκράτων (vulg. ἐσωκράτουν). This reading of the Ravenna MS. is rightly followed by all later editors. Such intransitive verbs in αω derived from nouns express 'having the affection indicated by the noun.'

1286. The translator suggests that ἄμ' ἂν is probably the true reading here (vulg. ἄμα). Cobet's emendation ἂν ἐνέμοντ' for ἀπενέμοντ' in v. 1289 is accepted, and it is noticeable that ἂν precedes its verb in each instance.

1299. ὑπ' ὀρτυγοκόπου. This reading, from the Scholiast, is generally adopted for the vulg. ὑπὸ στυφοκόμπου (στυφόκοπου), which, as Kock observes, may perhaps be equivalent in sense.

1338. For ἂν ποταθείην Shilleto conjectures ἀμποταθείην.

1340. ψευδαγγελήσειν, Bentley, &c. (vulg. ψευδαγγελὴς εἶν').

1344. καὶ πέτεσθαι βούλομαι οἰκῶν μεθ' ὑμῶν, K. conj. (vulg. καὶ πέτομαι καὶ βούλομαι οἰκεῖν μεθ' ὑμῶν).

1367. τὸν πατέρα δ' ἔα ζῆν, M. H. (vulg. τὸν πατέρ' ἔα ζῆν).

1376. φρενὸς ὄμματι γενειάν, Herm. &c. (vulg. φρενὶ σώματι τε νέαν).

1389. ἀέρια καὶ σκοτεινά, B. H. (vulg. ἀέρια καὶ σκότιά γε).

1395. ἀλάδε δρόμον, Herm. &c. (vulg. ἀλαδρόμον).

1407. Κρεκοπίδα (vulg. Κεκροπίδα). This conjecture of Kock, though not placed in his text, appears to the translator so highly probable, that he has followed it in his version. See footnote.

1410. ὄρνιθές τινες, Dind., &c. (vulg. ὄρνιθες τίνες).

1439. The vulgar text τοῖς μειρακίοις here is manifestly corrupt. Meineke conjectures and edits τοῖς φυλέταις. Kock conjectures τοῖς δημόταις, but leaves a blank in his text. Dobree's τῶν μειρακίων, which Holden has received, seems less probable than either of the others. No certainty can be obtained in such a case.

1496. τίς οὑγκαλυμμός, Dawes, &c. (vulg. τίς ὁ συγκαλυμμός;).

1506. ἀπὸ γάρ μ' ὀλεῖς, M. &c. (vulg. ἀπὸ γὰρ ὀλέσει μ', &c.).

1561. K. conjectures καθῆστο for ἀπῆλθεν, which seems corrupt. See footnote.

1582. ἐπικνῇ, Dobree from Schol. M. H. K. (vulg. ἐπικνῶ). This 'consensus' of editors is followed in the translation. Yet

APPENDIX B.

the use of ἀλλά suggests some question, whether the Indic. may not be the true reading. If so, then translate, '*I must scrape the silphium.*'

1656. νίθῳ 'ποθνῄσκων, K. (vulg. νοθεῖ' ἀποθνῄσκων). The true reading is, however, uncertain.

1681. For the corrupt reading βαδίζειν the conjectures are numerous: as, τιτυβίζει γ', βαβράζει γ', βαβάζει γ', βατίζει γ', βαΰζει γ', &c., any of which would be rendered '*twitters.*'

1731—42. The constitution of readings in this song is doubtful. In v. 1733 θεαί for vulg. θεοῖς is Brunck's conjecture adopted by M. H. and in the present translation. K. retains θεοῖς, but does not explain it. In v. 1732 τὸν for vulg. τῶν (a conjecture of Van Gent) is received by K. H.; but, as τὸν ἄρχοντα...μέγαν seems ungrammatical Greek, either Ζῆνα must be supplied afterwards or τῶν must be kept, ἄρχοντα being regarded as a substantive. For ἐν τοιῷδ' ὑμεναίῳ in v. 1735 and its antistrophic τῆς τ' εὐδαίμονος Ἥρας in v. 1741, M. and H. receive Dawes's emendations τοιῷδ' ὑμεναίῳ and κεὐδαίμονος Ἥρας. These corrections are uncertain, as the metrical change from initial anacrusis in the first three lines to base in the fourth is open to no objection. Ἐν does require correction on account of final quantity in v. 1734. Ζῆν' ἐν τῷδ' ὑμ. or Ζῆνα τῷδ' ὑμ. has occurred to the translator as possible, adopting τὸν in v. 1732.

1753. δία δὲ πάντα, Haupt, (vulg. διά σε τὰ πάντα).

1759. δάπεδον, M. (vulg. πέδον).

APPENDIX C.

Supplemental Notes.

I. *Peithetaerus.* p. 1.

This form of the name is (with Kock and Holden) preferred to the forms Peisthetaerus (MSS.), Peisetaerus (Dobree) and Pisthetaerus (Meineke). It is usually understood as meaning 'Persuader of a companion' (i.e. of Euelpides), 'Winmate' or 'Winfriend.' Köchly gives it a larger sense, 'Persuader of a hetaeria' (political club): and Donaldson calls the two Athenians Agitator and Hopegood. This interpretation is ingenious, but not certain.

II. *Cicalas.* p. 6.

42 (39). The cicala (tettix) was deemed by the Athenians an earthborn insect. Hence, as Thukydides tells us (1. 6), the wealthier citizens long wore golden grasshoppers in their hair as typical of their own indigenous character.

III. *Substitution or omission.* p. 16.

v. 143—9 (137—42). In this place, and in a few other passages, which a scholar reading will recognize, the translator has ventured to 'palliate' his author's grossness, by substituting for the thoughts and expressions of the Greek what seemed to be their nearest unobjectionable equivalents. The choice lay between this course and that of omission, by which the drama would be seriously mutilated, and would lose that completeness of form, which it is desirable to preserve.

IV. *The Four Birds.* p. 26.

v. 285—322 (207—304). The footnote is in accordance with Schönborn's views (*Die Skene der Hellenen*, p. 319). Prof. Wieseler of Göttingen, in his 'Adversaria,' argues at much length to shew that the four birds, which enter before the rest, were the musicians of the chorus, three (Flamingo, Hoopoe Minor and Gobbler) flute-players, the fourth (Medus) a lyre-player. They do not, in his opinion, come on the proskenium and retire again as mutes, but enter the orchestra at once by the right-hand parodos, and remain there near the chorus after its entrance, accompanying its songs with their instrumental music. This conjecture, which Kock seems to favour, is ingenious, and the reasons urged by its learned author are instructive, as when he urges that musicians were often foreigners, and that they wore bright dresses like these four birds. (See also Wieseler's *Theatergebäude* Tab. XIII. with his notes.) Yet it may be said, that we should have looked for some distinct allusion in the play itself to the musical character of these four birds, such as the nightingale and raven obtain. Nothing of this kind appears, except the problematic epithet 'museseer,' applied to the Medus-bird. This bird is in the footnote stated (with Kock and Droysen) to be a variety of the 'gallus gallinaceus,' afterwards called 'the Persian bird.' H. Müller (in his translation) denies this identity on account of the epithets 'exedros' (*holding an uncommon site*) 'atopos' (*absurd*), which, he says, would not have been applied to a bird so well known as the cock. There is much force in this objection. The term 'exedros' (*out of seat*) is augural, and proper to a prophetic bird viewed in an unusual (and therefore ill-boding) situation. Like 'museseer,' 'horsecock,' &c. it is taken from Aeschylus, and exemplifies the comic practice of parodying tragic phraseology.

V. *The Hoopoes of Sophokles and Philokles.* p. 29.

v. 229 (281). This passage must be considered in connexion with v. 106—7 (101—2). Schöll (*Sophokles*) denies that in either place the Hoopoe of Aristophanes identifies himself with that of

Sophokles, or that the Hoopoe of Philokles is to be regarded as the grandson of the Sophoklean bird. He argues, from the verses 106—7 (101—2) that *The Tereus* of Sophokles must have been acted shortly before *The Birds;* but that *The Pandionis* (a tetralogy) of Philokles, which gained the prize against *The Oedipus Rex* of Sophokles (!), must be ascribed to B. C. 431. If we allow the latter date to be probable (though not certain), we need not grant that *The Tereus* was certainly acted for the first time shortly before *The Birds*, on account of the lines above cited of this play. A drama of Sophokles would live long in the minds of Athenians, nor was the immediate recollection of the audience requisite to justify the allusion there. Neither are jests like that now before us to be pressed to all their consequences. Aristophanes wants to say two things; that the Hoopoe of Philokles is a scrubby bird, and that it is a type of the profligate Kallias. For this purpose he uses the Athenian custom of naming sons from their grandparents, and so he is obliged to make his own Hoopoe father of Philokles, in order to make him also grandfather of Hoopoe Minor. But whether the Scholiast is right in saying that the Aristophanic Hoopoe is identified with the Sophoklean, or Schöll in maintaining the contrary opinion, there is not evidence enough to determine.

VI. *The Crest.* p. 30.

v. 309 (291). On the various meanings of the word 'lophos' see Liddell and Scott's Lexicon. As a crest, it may consist of feathers, or of horsehair, or of flesh, as the cock's comb. But there is no evidence to support the strange notion of Wieseler that the 'lophoi' of the birds here imply a kind of sandals.

VII. *The term Parodos, and the Positions of the Chorus.* p. 32.

v. 281 (263). The term 'Parodos,' as applied to the Greek drama, is used with four varieties of meaning. (1) It is primarily applied to the two passages (parodoi) leading into the orchestra between the stage-buildings (skenê) and the extremities of the 'koilon' or 'theatre' proper, where the spectators sat. Wieseler

APPENDIX C.

(*Griechenland*, IV. note 225) combats this statement, here adopted, of Schönborn and Buttmann, contending that the 'parodoi' were doors opening on the stage itself through walls in the side scenes near the 'periacti' or machinery. (2) Parodos signifies the entrance of the chorus into the orchestra. (3) Parodos gives name to the ode sung by the chorus on its first entrance (this does not occur in *The Birds*.) (4) Parodos expresses that portion of a comedy, which contains the approach of the chorus, its entrance, and all that intervenes before it settles down (so to speak) to its regular duties in the drama. This portion is of great length in *The Birds*, extending from v. 281 (263) to v. 470 (450).

In this (as in most comedies) the 24 choreutae enter the orchestra (by the right-hand parodos) in six rows of four each, the coryphaeus being nearest the spectators in the third row. The temporary arrangement for their accommodation, varying probably in different dramas, is to a great extent conjectural. We suppose it to have been a wooden platform, extending from the 'thymele' (altar of Dionysus) to the 'proskenium' or stage, which it bordered to some extent, being somewhat below it. It was ascended, perhaps, by two flights of steps, one on each side of the 'thymele,' and would have steps connecting it with the stage. During the Epeisodia, which occupy the greater part of the drama, the chorus stood facing the stage in four rows of six choreutae each (perhaps with a double central interval shewing two semichoruses), the coryphaeus again being third from the left hand in the hindmost row, next the spectators. When a stasimon or antistrophic ode was sung, they formed themselves into two semichoruses, standing opposite one another (antiprosôpon), each semichorus in three rows of four: and then each had its own coryphaeus, facing one another next to the spectators. In order to perform the Parabasis, the chorus simply wheeled round from its 'epeisodic' position so as to front the theatre, and probably advanced to the outer rim of the platform. Thus the chief coryphaeus would be in the front row, third from the (spectators') left, and it is supposed that now the second coryphaeus was next upon his left hand. Thus again were formed two semichoruses, not face to face, but side by side. According to Hermann and Arnoldt, in a full Parabasis, the first coryphaeus sang the 'kommation,' and recited the Parabasis proper with its 'pnigos:' then the first semichorus sang the ode or strophe; then the first coryphaeus recited the epirrhema; then the second semichorus sang the antode or antistrophe: and finally the second coryphaeus recited the antepirrhema: after which the chorus wheeled back into its epeisodic position fronting the stage[1].

[1] In Donaldson's *Theatre of the Greeks* (Ed. 7, p. 229), the orchestral arrangements are thus described: "The orchestra was a levelled space twelve feet lower than the front seats of the 'koilon,' by which it was bounded. *Six feet* above this was a boarded stage, which did not cover the whole area of the orchestra, but terminated where the line of view from the central 'cunei' was intercepted by the boundary line. It ran however to the right and left of the spectators' benches *till it reached the sides of the scene*. The main part of this platform, as well as an altar of Bacchus in the centre of the orchestral circle, was called the 'thymele.' The segment of the orchestra not covered by this platform was the 'konistra,' arena, or place of sand. In front of the elevated scene and *six feet* higher than the platform in the orchestra (*i.e.* on the same level with the lowest range of seats) was the 'proscenium,' called also the 'logeion' or speaking-stage. There was a double flight of steps from the arena to the platform in the orchestra, and another of a similar description from the orchestral platform to the 'proscenium' or real stage.

In a footnote on the term 'thymele' is added:

"The student should remark the successive extensions of meaning with which this word is used. At first it signified the altar of Bacchus, round which the cyclic chorus danced the dithyramb. *Then it signified the platform on which this altar stood, and which served for the limited evolutions of the chorus. Lastly it denoted any platform* (?)......We believe that in the time of Euripides, at all events, the 'thymele' signified the platform for the chorus, and not merely the altar *which stood upon it*."

The points in this description from which we dissent are marked by italics. The last words *which stood upon it* seem to be a mere oversight, as the 'thymele' stood, no doubt, on its own low platform or pedestal of marble, in the centre of the 'konistra' or orchestral floor. Its summit probably filled a scoop in the temporary woodwork of the choral platform, and on either side of it rose to that platform the 'klimakteres' or double flight of steps by which the two semichoruses severally reached their

VIII. *The Division of* Choral Parts. p. 33.

v. 327—467 (310—447). A controversy exists among German scholars respecting the parts given to the several choreutae in song and recitation. According to Bamberger, Hermann, Ritschl and others, a division of parts between them was made. Rossbach and Westphal, with other scholars, hold that, while the coryphaeus took the dialogue and recitative parts, the melic passages were sung by the rest of the chorus: but these critics do not always agree in their results, owing to the difficulty of distinguishing accurately between what was recited and what was sung. Arnoldt, the latest writer on this question, defends Hermann's view: and, treating of this Parodos, he distributes the choral parts between the 24 choreutae (including the coryphaeus), assigning also to the coryphaeus what belongs to him exclusively. Whether this distribution be exact or not, it is ingenious and interesting; for which reason it is added here, the Greek lines being cited, but the words of the English translation indicated.

Choreut. α′   v. 310   Wh— wh— ......he?
—   β′   — 315   T— T—............say?
—   γ′   — 319   Where? ....say?

station. Again, it seems probable that the choral platform was nine or ten feet above the floor of the orchestra, *i.e.* three or two feet only lower than the stage. How, for instance, could the scene in the Parodos of this drama, where the birds prepare to assail the two Athenians, be effectively represented, if the 'choreutae' stood so far below the actors? Lastly, how could the choral platform be extended so far to the right and left as *to reach the sides of the scene?* In that case it must have blocked up the 'parodoi,' leaving no room for the entrance and march of the Chorus. According to our conception, it flanked the 'logeion' or central space of the proskenium. Its size we cannot state exactly, but it would be large enough for the standing-room and evolutions of the Chorus, perhaps also for its instrumentalists, unless these were in the 'konistra.' Thus room would be left for the Chorus (and others?) to enter the orchestra by the 'parodoi.' A chorus entering by the right-hand parodos, as in *The Birds*, would then turn to its left, and, going round the platform as far as the 'thymele,' would ascend to its station in two equal divisions.

—	δ′	— 322—3	O you ....deed ?
—	ε′	— 325	So you've ....done it ?
—	ϛ′	— 326	And are ....near us?
—	ζ′	— 327—32	Alas, alas ! ....is breaking ;
—	η′	— 333—5	Lures me ....to be.
—	θ′	— 336—8	But we ....by us.
—	ι′	— 343—8	Ho! forward! ...supply.
—	ια′	— 349—51	For nor ....from me.
—	ιβ′	— 352—3	So let us............our right.
—	ιγ′	— 364	Eleleleu ....for delay ;
—	ιδ′	— 365	Haul 'em ....away.
—	ιε′	— 369—70	Spare them ? ......kind ?
—	ιϛ′	— 373—4	Can it be ....of old ?
—	ιζ′	— 381—2	Well, indeed ......teach.
—	ιη′	— 383	Ne'er on............to you.
Coryphaeus.		— 400—6	Now again.........what ho !
—	———	— 408	Who are............tell us.
—	———	— 410—2	To the birds ......brings 'em.
Chor.	ιθ′	— 414	What's this ......tell?
—	κ′	— 415	What proposals...make ?
—	κα′	— 417	Sees he ....to defend ?
—	κβ′	— 427	What ?........ ......fool?
—	κγ′	— 429	Has he...............or two ?
—	κδ′	— 432—4	His proposals......flutter.

The next following choral speeches belong to the coryphaeus (see 'Die Chorpartieen bei Aristophanes' von Dr Richard Arnoldt). Arnoldt lays it down as a rule of Greek Comedy, that the actor on the stage is never addressed, *conversationally*, by the united song of the chorus, but either (usually) by their leader, the coryphaeus, or, in 'kommatic' passages, such as the one above cited (vv. 310—434), by individual choreutae, to whom the several 'kommata' are distributed. And he draws special attention to the fact that, where a Chorikon sung by the chorus does appear addressed to the actor, it is at once followed by a few verses which, as it were, sum it up and point it practically; which verses, he says, are addressed to the actor by the coryphaeus. Such an instance occurs in the Chorikon next following the passage already cited, vv. 471—484 (451—461): where the words, 'At every time...... shall be,' are sung by the full chorus, addressing Peithetaerus, but *not conversationally*, while the two following verses, 'So, whatever......broken,' are spoken to him *conversationally* by the coryphaeus, who invites him to commence his speech. Similar conclusions, ascribed to the coryphaeus, are vv. 578—9, (548—9), 'Forthwith then......reclaim.' vv. 668—9 (636—7), 'All the work ...mind.' vv. 1274—6 (1196—8), 'Look out—...nigh.'

That the tetrameters and trimeters in the 'Epeisodia,' ascribed to the chorus, were spoken by the coryphaeus, is obvious.

In the 'amoebean' passage, vv. 1394—1419 (1313—1336), 'Ere long......lazy loon,' the melic verses ascribed to the chorus were, in Arnoldt's opinion, chanted by the coryphaeus.

In the Exodos, vv. 1721—1765, Arnoldt assigns to the coryphaeus the opening and concluding chants, 'Room for the company.......Royalty,' and 'Taralala......deity.' The strophe and antistrophe of the first song, 'When the goddess Fates' &c., were, he says, sung each by a semi-chorus. The second song, 'O the mighty' &c., was sung by the full chorus. He ascribes to Peithetaerus the words, 'Stay yet......Zeus the king.' As regards the two songs he is certainly right. Perhaps, too, he is right in giving to the coryphaeus the first passage, though it is quite possible that the chorus and coryphaeus divided it between them, the chorus beginning, and the coryphaeus following at 'Great fortune'....... But there is no sufficient reason for confining the final words, 'Taralala, &c.' to the coryphaeus only, when they seem in most respects much more appropriate to the musical outburst of the entire chorus. Nor, again, do the words, 'Stay yet a little while' &c., appear suited to the mouth of Peithetaerus. They are more fitly chanted by the coryphaeus[1].

---

[1] We are inclined, with some critics, to reject the words ἐχάρην ᾠδαῖς as a gloss.

IX. *Adjuration of Animals and Trees.* p. 53.

v. 548 (521). Instead of referring this Greek custom to the cause suggested in the note, some scholars may be inclined to derive it from the primeval practice of animal worship and tree worship. See Sir J. Lubbock's *Origin of Civilization,* ch. v.; also Fergusson's *Tree and Serpent Worship.*

X. *Footpads and Cloak Robbers.* p. 69.

v. 749 (712). Müller-Strübing (*Aristophanes und die Historische Kritik,* p. 29, &c.) considers 'Orestes' to be a general cant name for footpads of the time. He observes also, that this crime of cloak-thieving or highway-robbery is mentioned thrice in *The Birds,* but not in any other play of Aristophanes. Hence he concludes that (like 'garotting' in London some few years since) it was an outbreak of a disturbed period, and a temporary mischief only. In the passage of the *Acharnians,* v. 1160, &c., he thinks a street-brawl is described, not a robbery, and supposes the term there ('some Orestes') to describe a tipsy violent street-reveller, like the 'Mohawks' of London in the early part of the 18th century.

XI. *The Hermokopidae and the 'Popish Plot.'*

The remarkable parallel between the affair of the Hermokopidae at Athens, B.C. 415, and the Popish Plot of 1678 in England, has been pointed out by Bishop Thirlwall and Mr Grote. It may be seen in the following particulars.

I. In Athens (1) the Hetaeries secretly conspired to destroy Alkibiades, and to promote a revolution in favour of oligarchic principles: (2) their plan was, to fanaticise the people, and to direct public indignation against impiety and profanation of things religious: (3) for this purpose they availed themselves of a crime, the mutilation of the Hermae : (4) and the inquiry into this crime they extended to an inquisition of all malpractices against religion, offering rewards for evidence : (5) agents of theirs, supported by the priests and soothsayers, accused Alkibiades in the Ekklesia of such malpractices, and endeavoured to depose him from the office of commander, but failed for a time : (6) a crowd of witnesses, more or less dishonest and false, came forward to inculpate him and many other persons : (7) in consequence of which some were put to death, others fled : (8) among the witnesses was one of the Hermokopidae (Andokides), who, under the stress of fear, confessed a part at least of the truth, and so caused the condemnation of his own friends : (9) the historical consequences were, that the Hetaeries or oligarchic party became so far successful that they deposed and expelled Alkibiades, and within a few years established an oligarchy, soon defeated and punished : they came back to power when Athens was captured, but were again defeated and crushed by the expulsion of the Thirty, and the Democracy was permanently restored : (10) the general result being, that popular principles triumphed in Athens.

II. In England (1) the popular party, led by Shaftesbury, and having the support of the House of Commons, conspired to exclude James Duke of York from succession to the throne, to control the royal power, and to promote a revolution in favour of civil and religious liberty : (2) their plan was, to fanaticise the people, and to direct public indignation against 'Popery,' and 'Papists,' especially against 'Popish priests:' (3) for this purpose they availed themselves of a crime, the murder, or supposed murder, of Sir Edmundsbury Godfrey : (4) and the inquiry into this crime they extended to an inquisition of all treasons imputed to 'Papists' and 'Popish priests,' offering rewards for evidence : (5) their supporters in the Commons inculpated the Duke of York and his household, and passed a Bill to exclude him from succession, but were thwarted by the firmness of the King, and the defeat of their Bill in the House of Peers : (6) a crowd of witnesses, more or less dishonest and false (Oates, Bedloe, Dangerfield, &c.), came forward to accuse persons of all classes : (7) in consequence of which many were put to death, many imprisoned and persecuted in various ways, and some went into exile: (8) when the tide had turned against the popular party, one of its members (Lord Howard of Escrick), under the stress of fear, appeared as a witness against his friends, and so caused the condemnation of Lord Russell and others: (9) the historical consequences were, that, after much cruelty and injustice inflicted on Roman Catholics, Charles II. contrived to baffle the popular party, and to turn the tables on them: whereby they suffered great misfortunes in his reign and in that of his successor, many being executed, many driven into exile; till at length, through his own blind folly, James II. lost his throne, and the civil and religious liberties of England were secured by the transfer of the crown to William of Orange-Nassau and Mary his wife: (10) the general result being, that popular principles triumphed in England[1].

It has been often said, that History repeats itself: and the striking parallelism of these events, in such distant times, and in countries so differently situated in most respects, is a verification of that saying. Among the lessons which it is calculated to teach, are these two:

First: that the crime of pursuing political ends by wicked means, of doing evil that a supposed good may come, is not confined to any party, but has been committed by all parties in turn, absolutist, oligarchic and democratic, even to our own days; and the deduction is, that factious party-spirit is a vice so deeply rooted in human nature, that the warnings of history have failed, and may long fail, to correct it.

---

[1] The only inexactness in this parallel is, that in England the first deposition concerning 'the Popish plot' was anterior to the death of Godfrey, having indeed been sworn before him as a magistrate. That event, however, was at once used to spread and strengthen popular fanaticism; and many of those arrested were tried and convicted as principals or accomplices in the murder.

Secondly: that religion, the use of which is to convert men from evil to good, has in all times, and in all its forms, been abused to uncharitable, unjust and unholy ends: and the deduction is, not that religion itself is bad, but that 'the corruption of that which is best is worst,' and therefore most of all to be condemned, dreaded and avoided both by nations and by individuals.

www.ingramcontent.com/pod-product-compliance
Lightning Source LLC
Chambersburg PA
CBHW031742230426
43669CB00007B/449